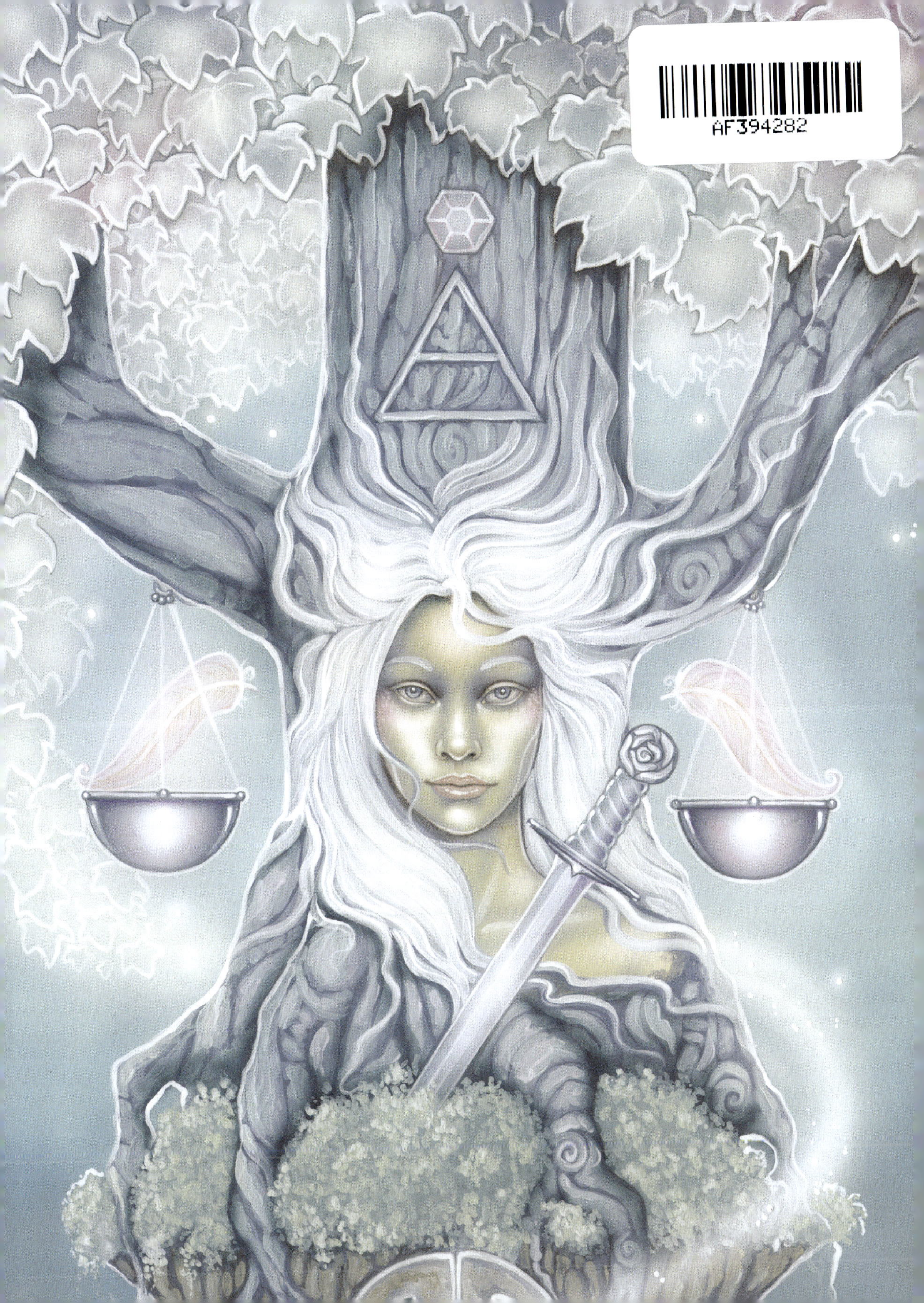
AF394282

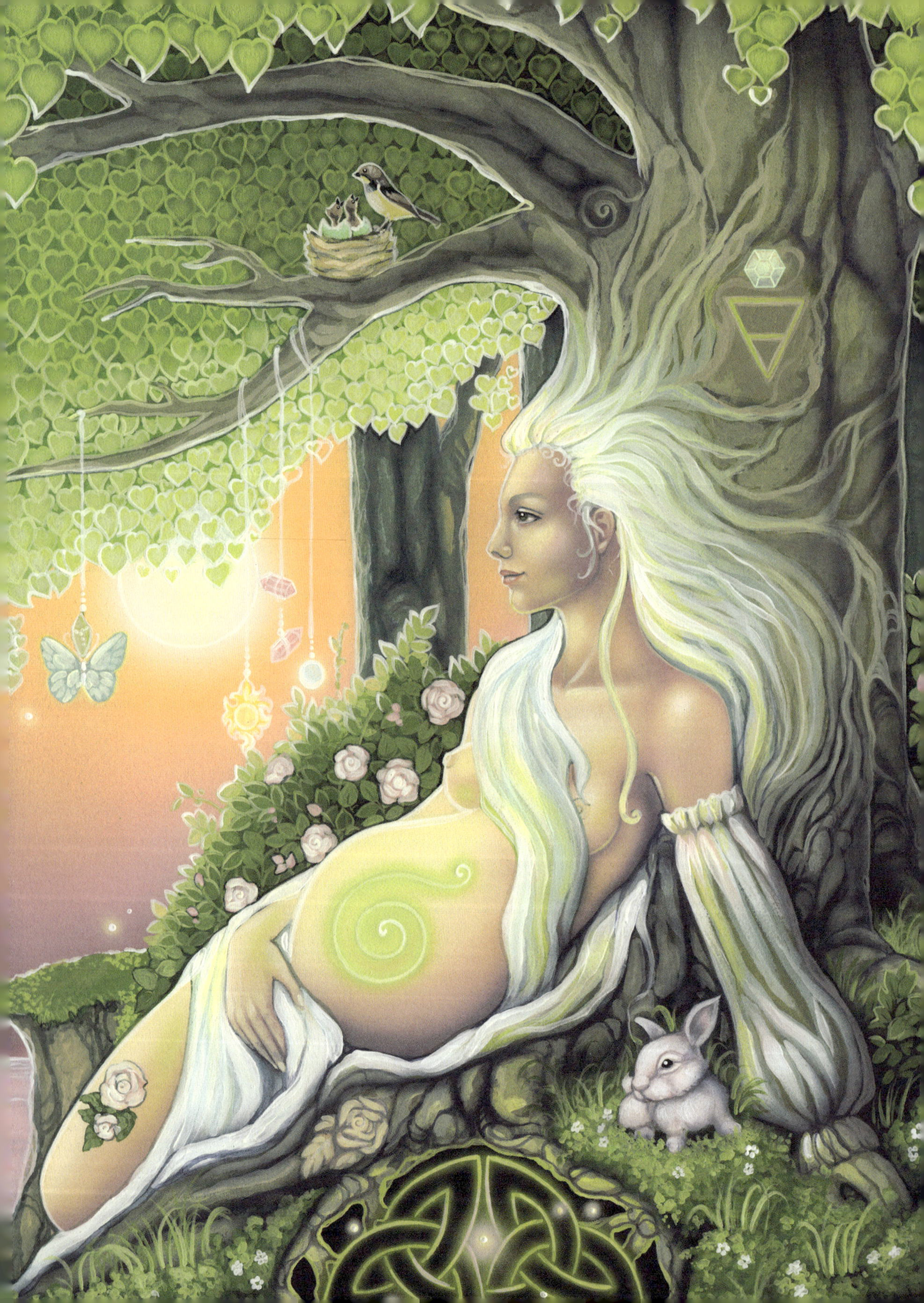

This journal belongs to

Love ...

A gift from the Divine.

Like the gentle wings of a butterfly,

It dwells at the centre of our being.

Bright, pure, soft, fragile,

And yet infinite and eternal.

It is the seed of potential –

The heart of creation –

And to create is to know the Divine.

Love ...

It is a spark, a seed of light,

Planted within us when our soul was birthed.

Hold the spark of Love close,

Let it guide you to your true purpose,

Let it become a beacon to others –

Those whose light may falter.

Let it be your one true reason for being.

Love ...

A source of Strength,

A source of Hope,

A pathway to Divinity,

A path that leads you home.

– Ravynne Phelan

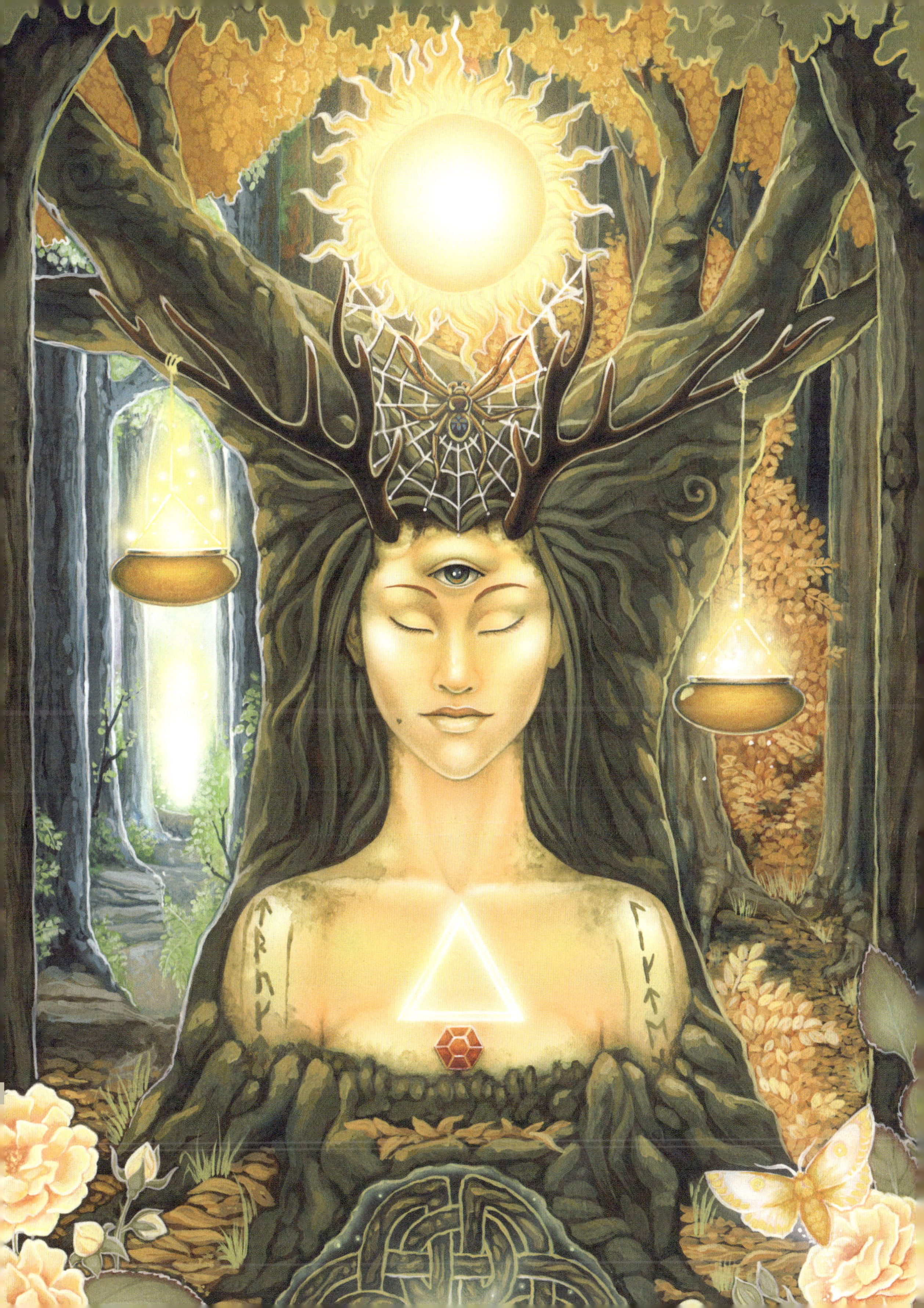

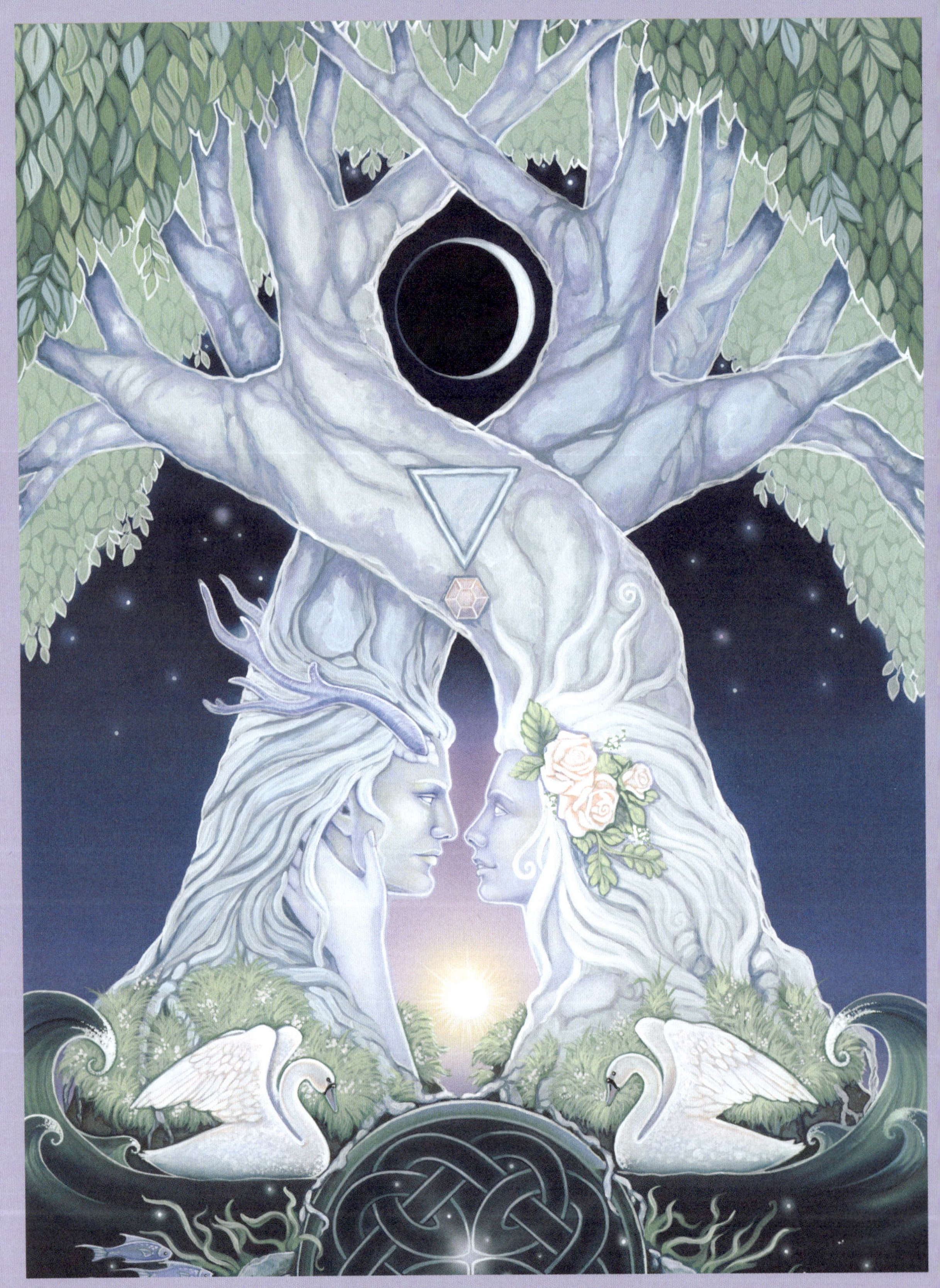

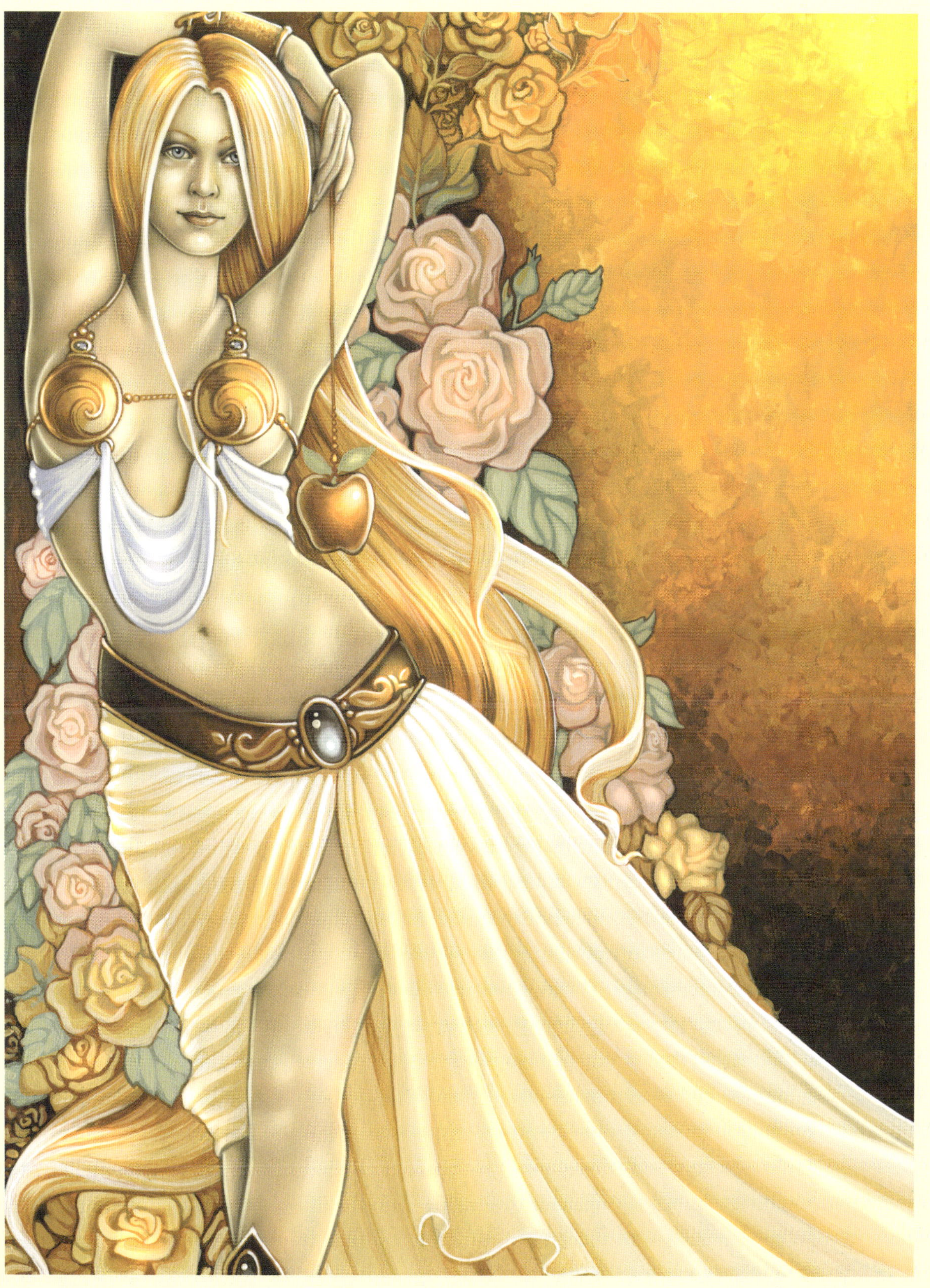

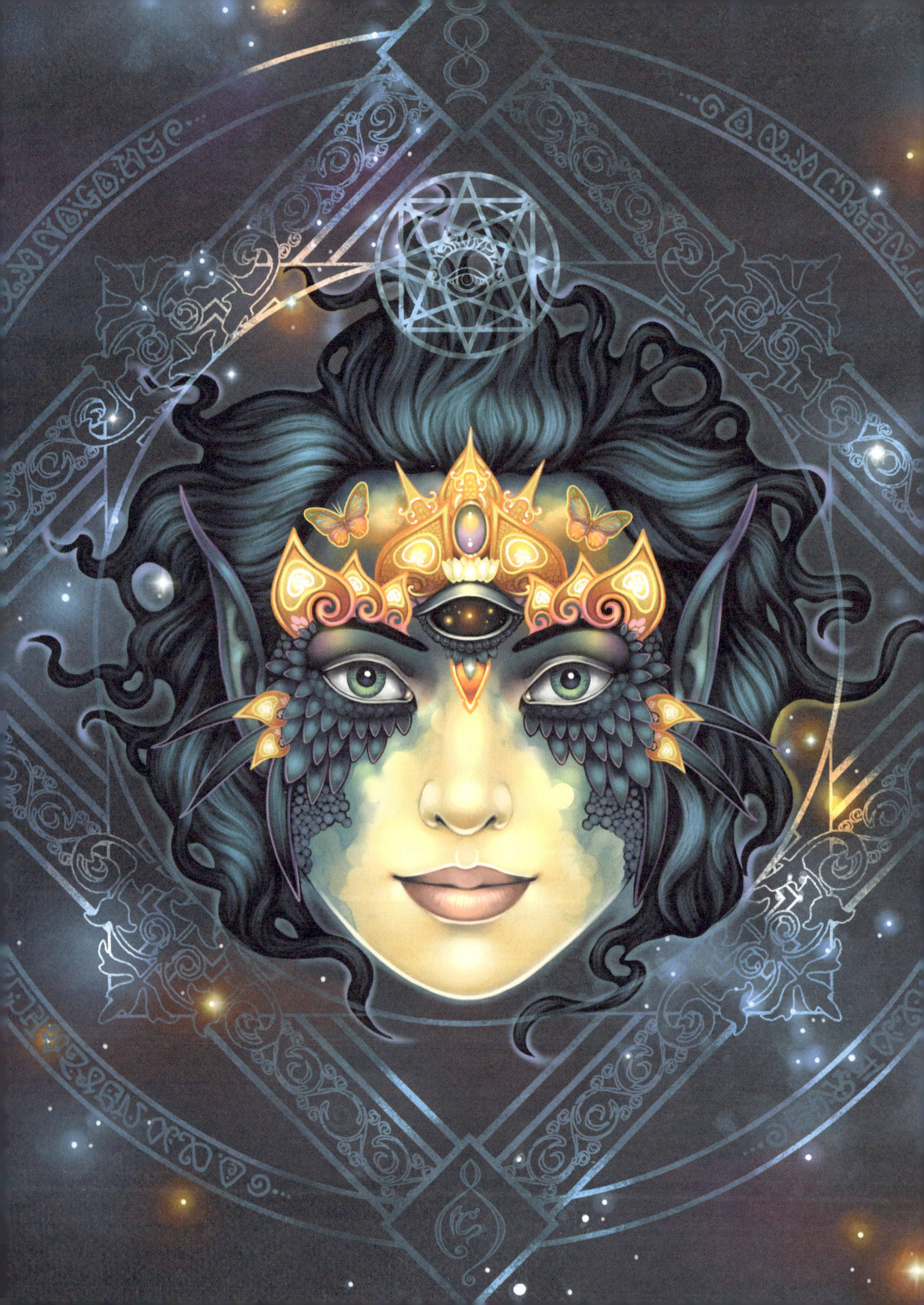

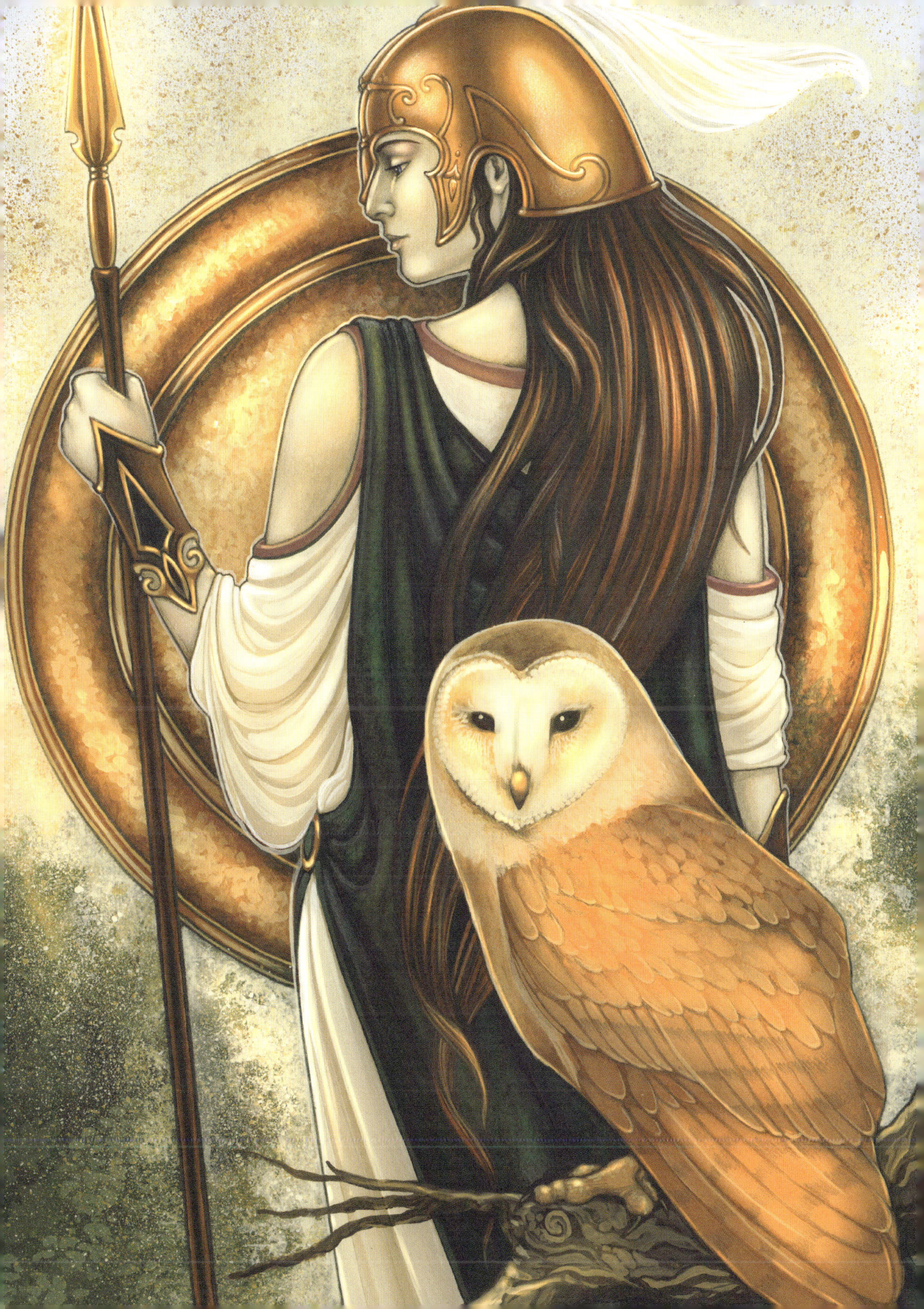

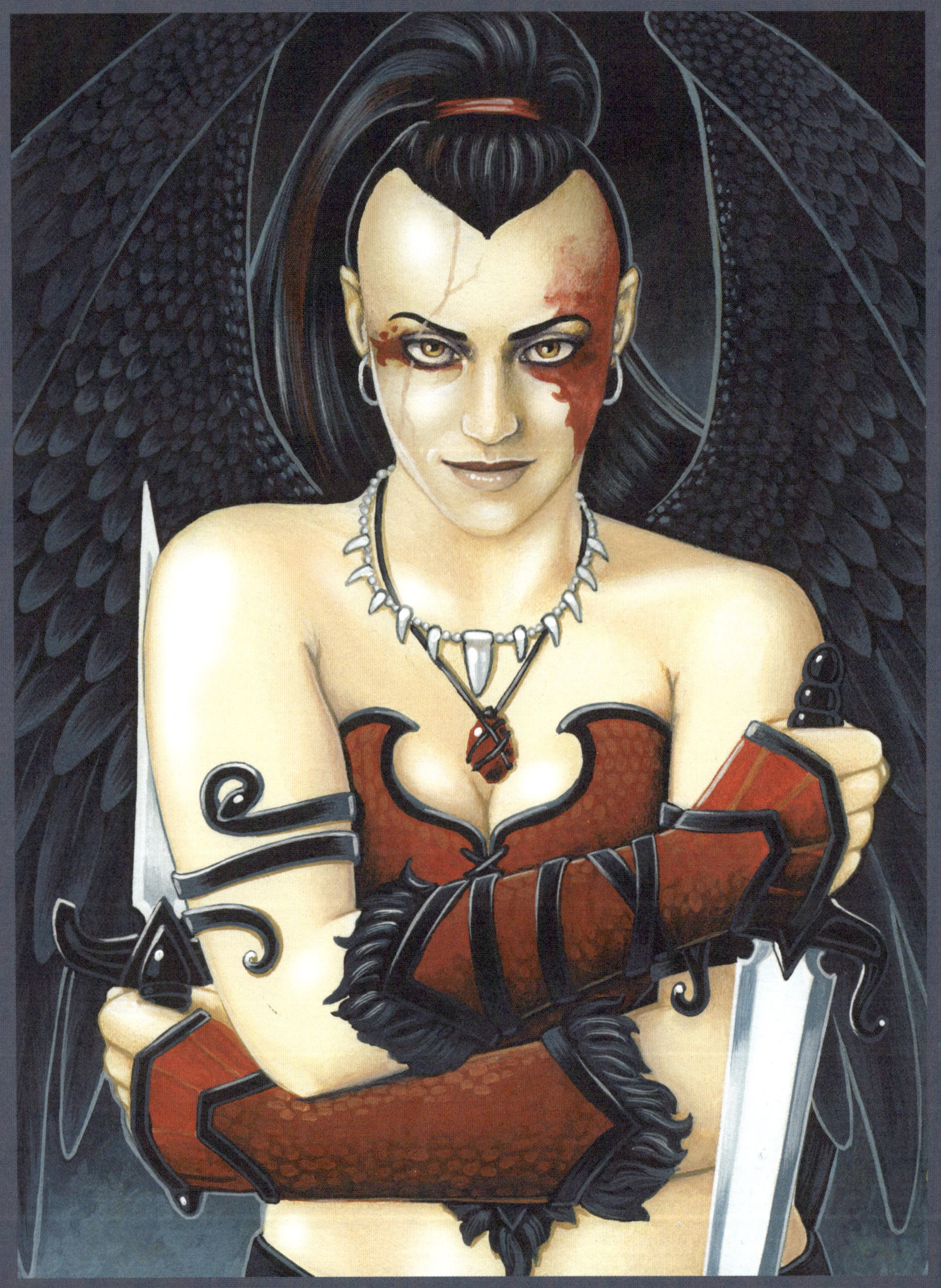

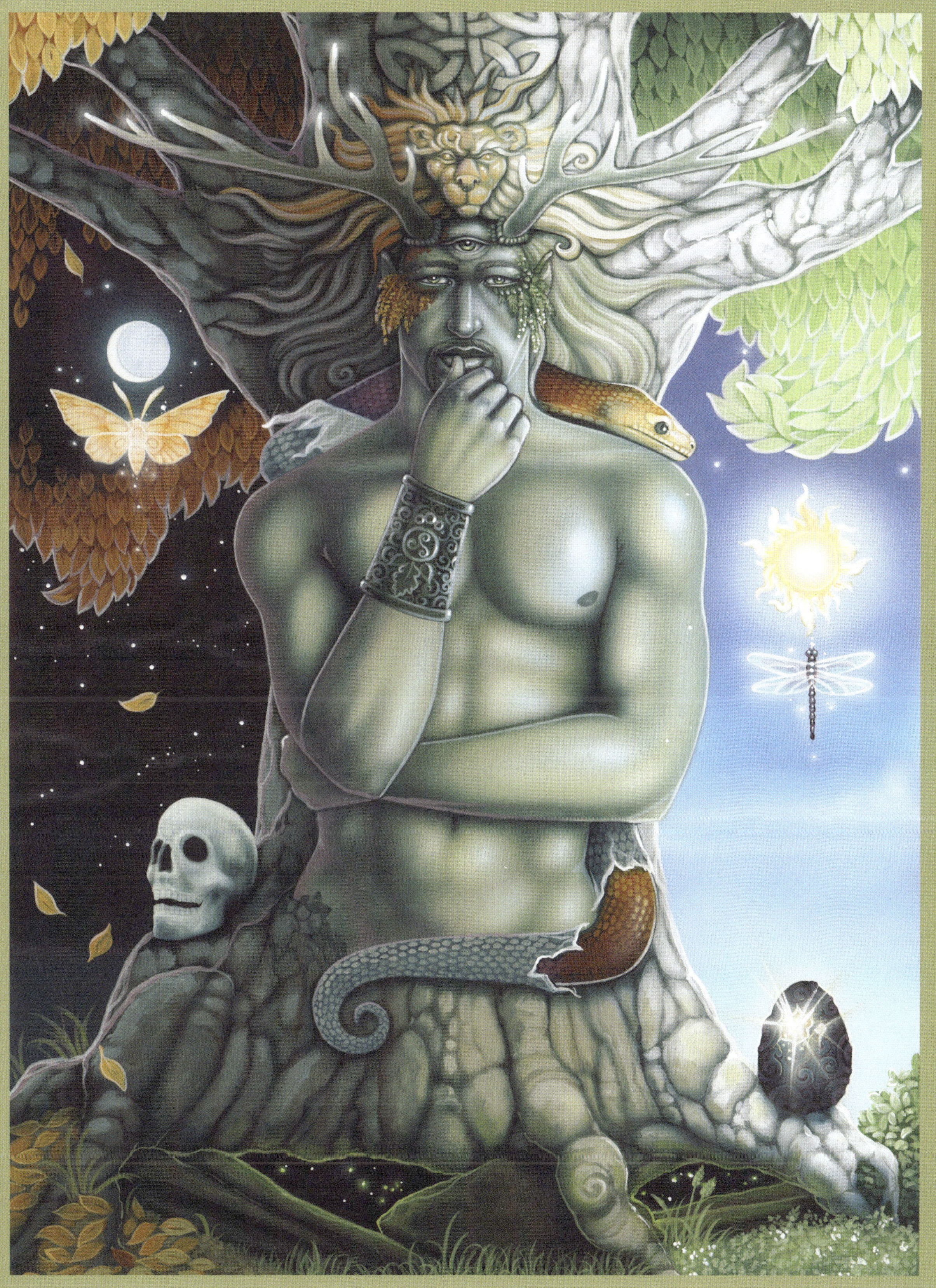

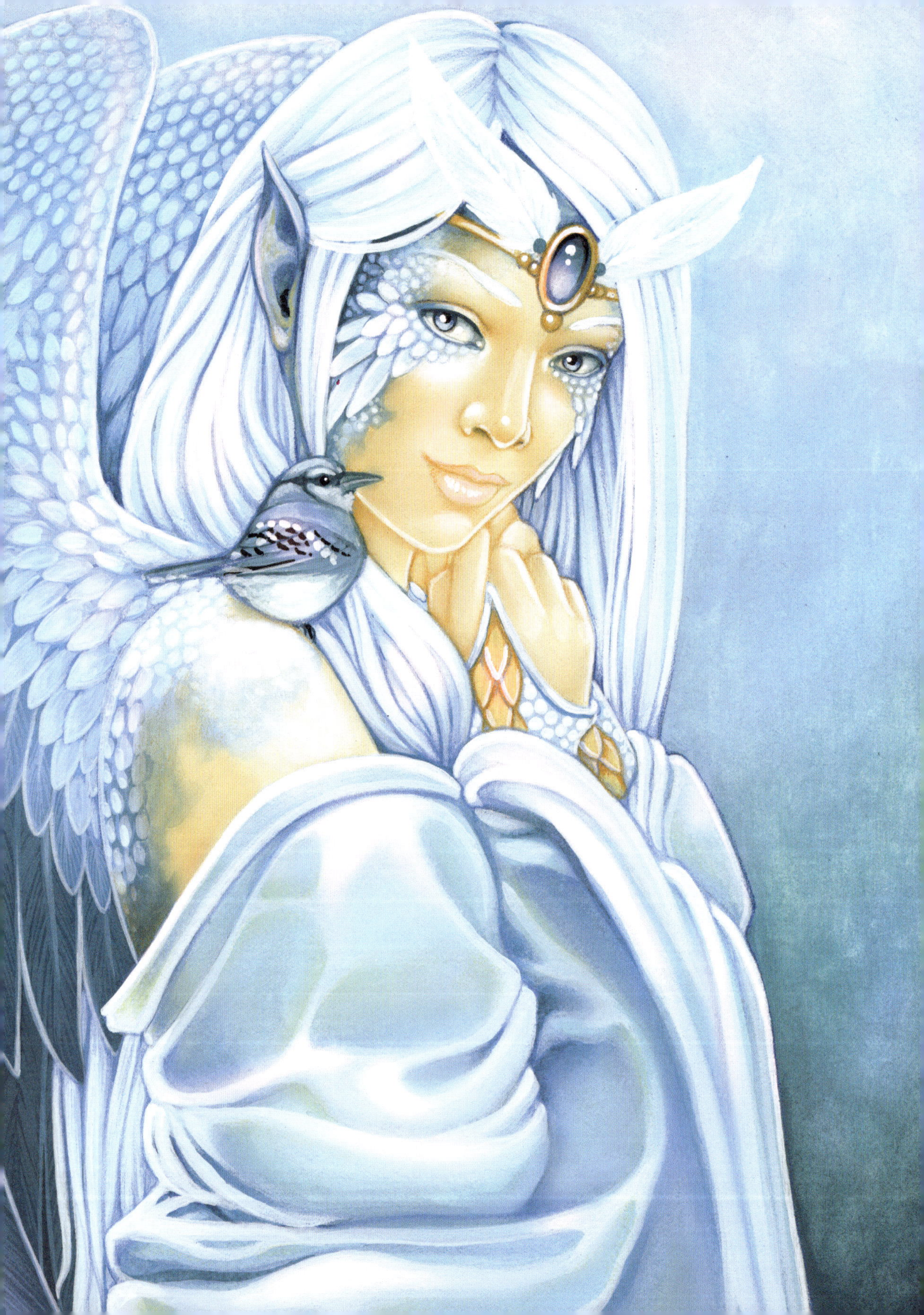

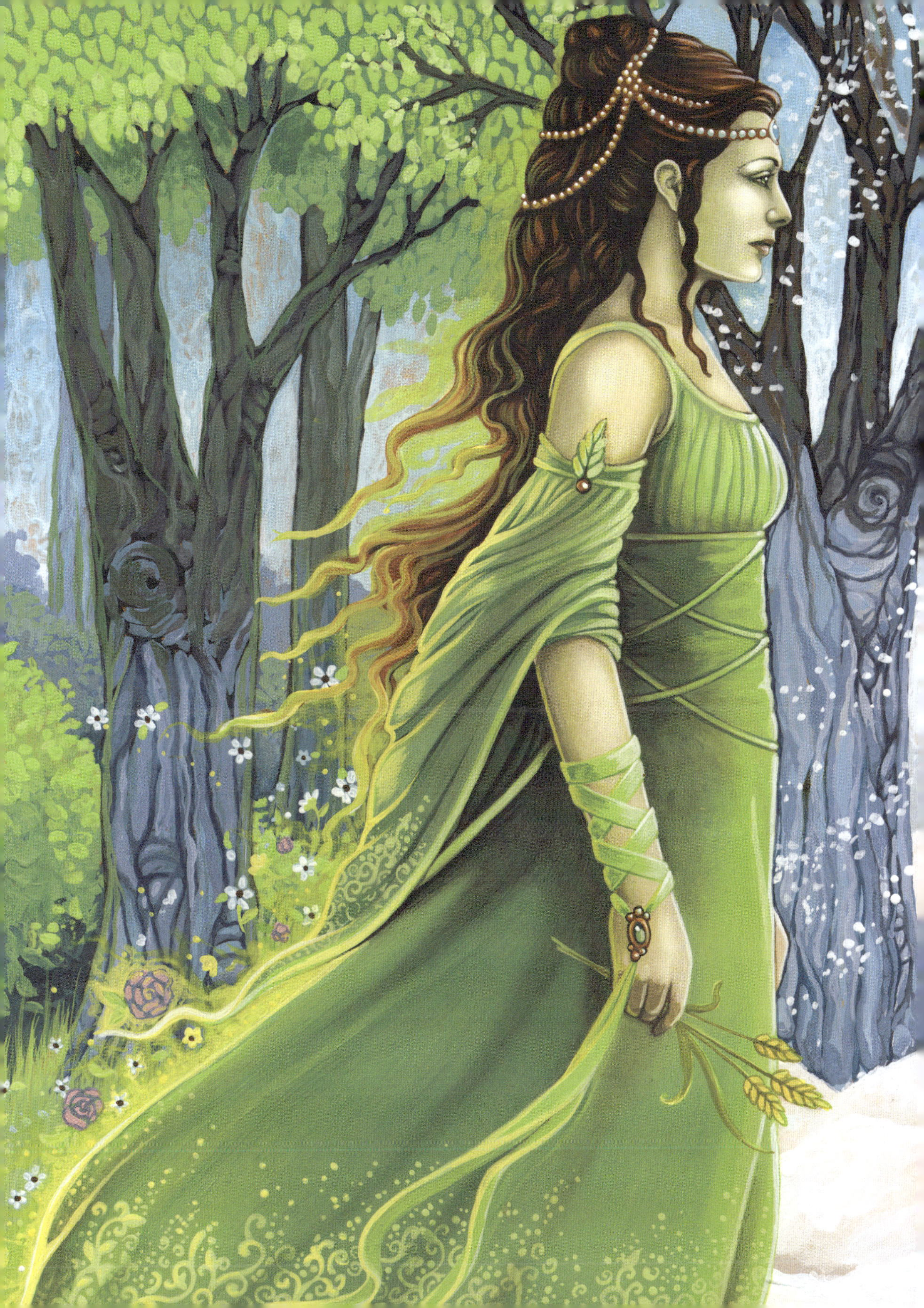

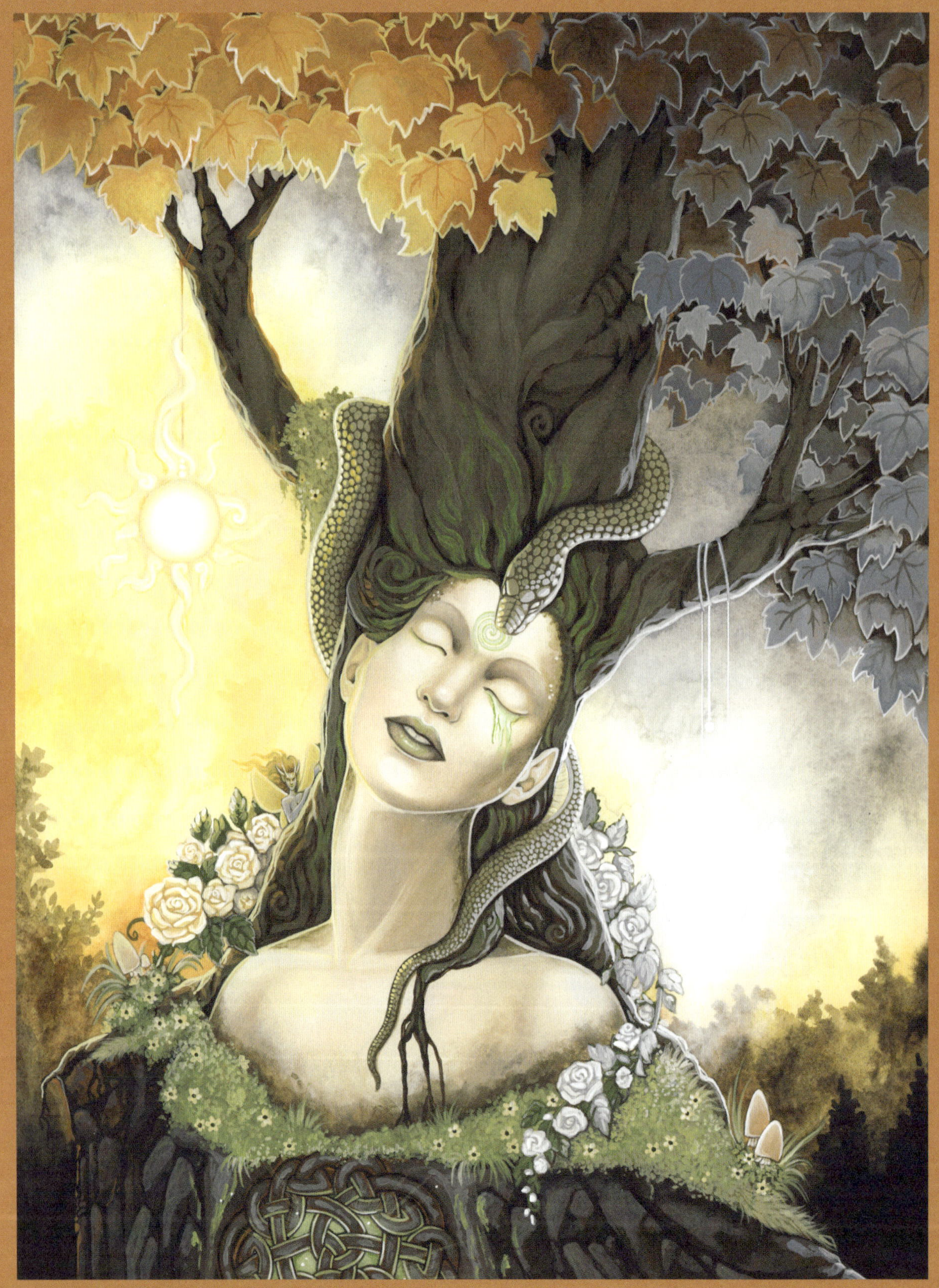

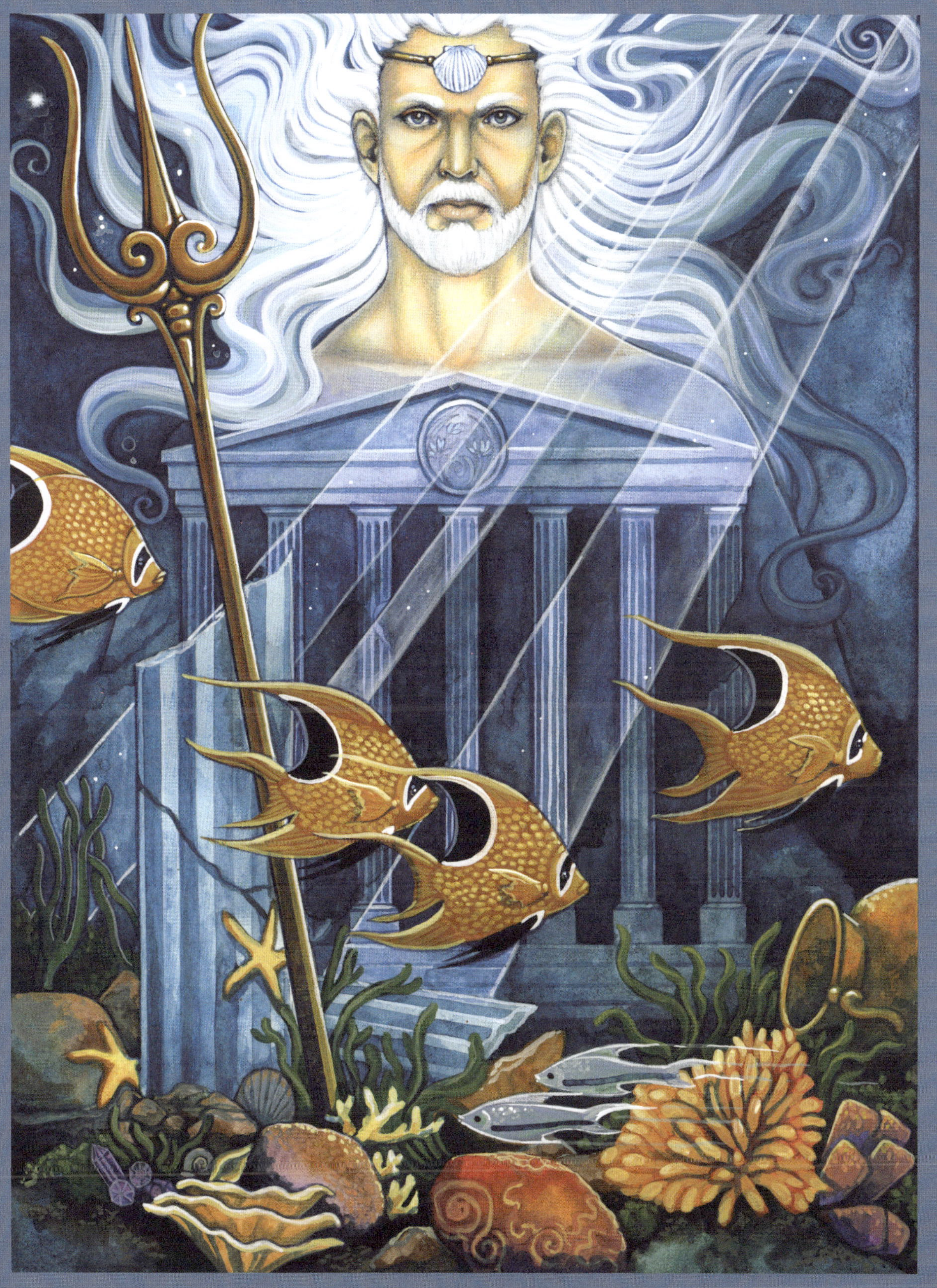

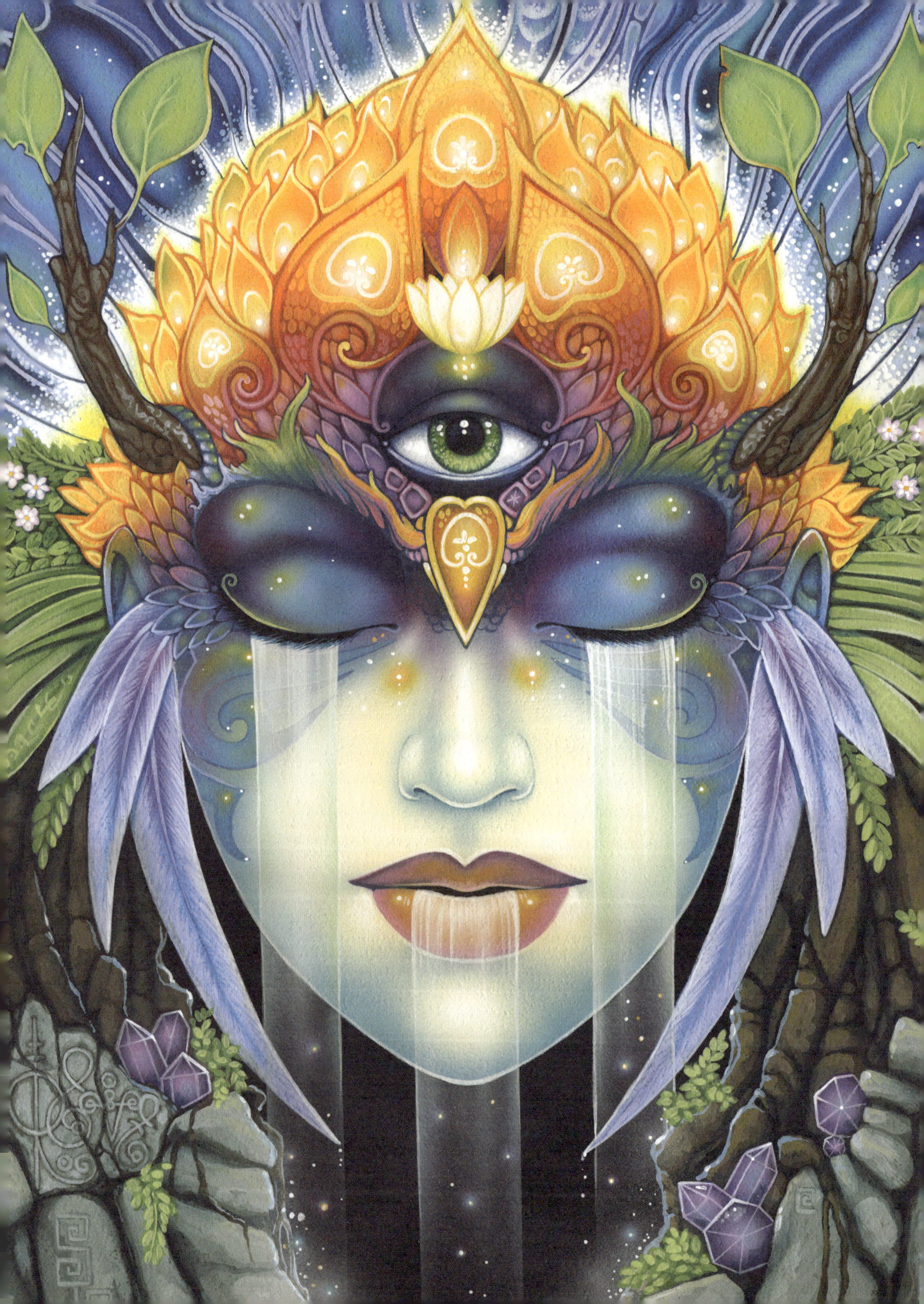

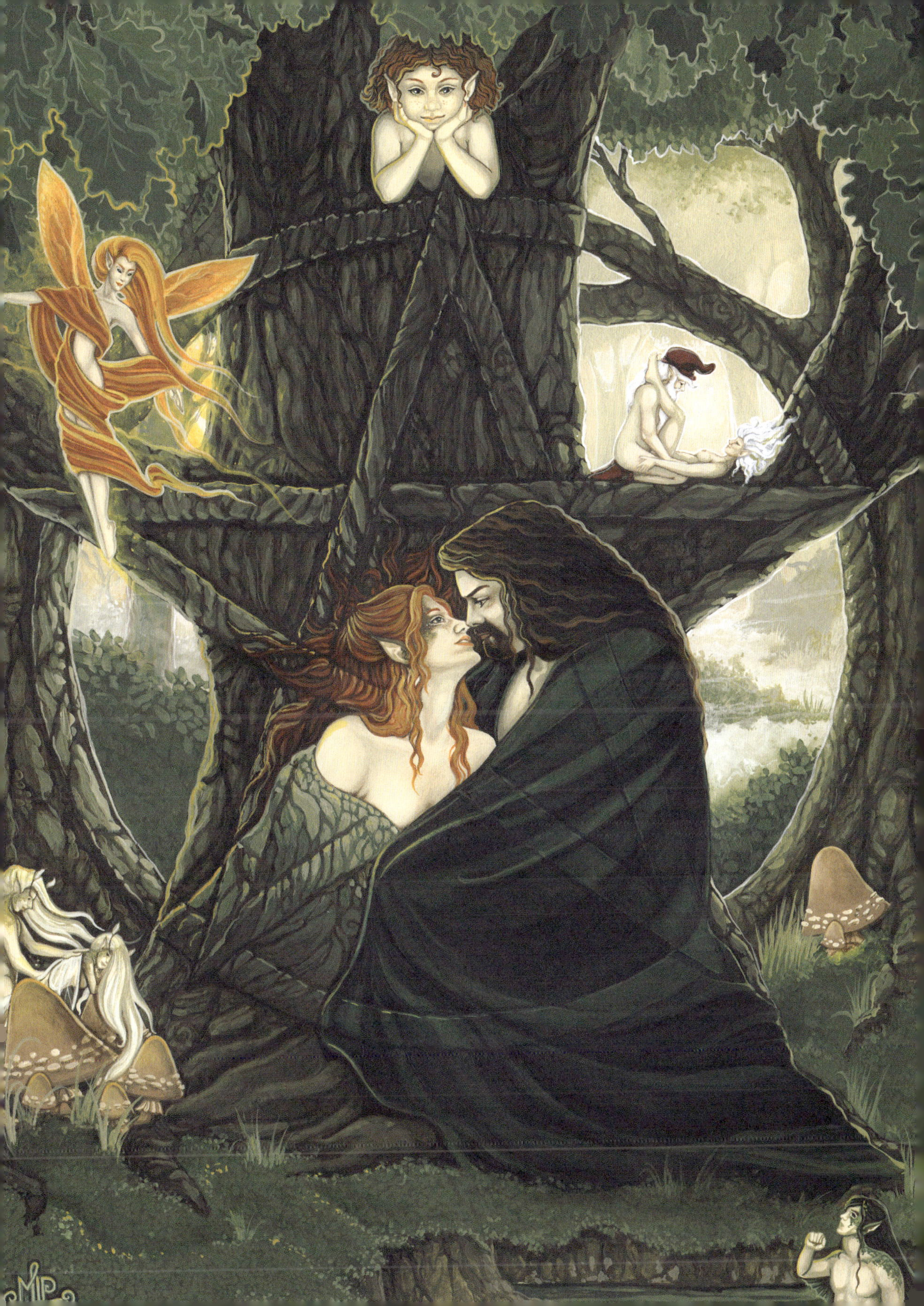

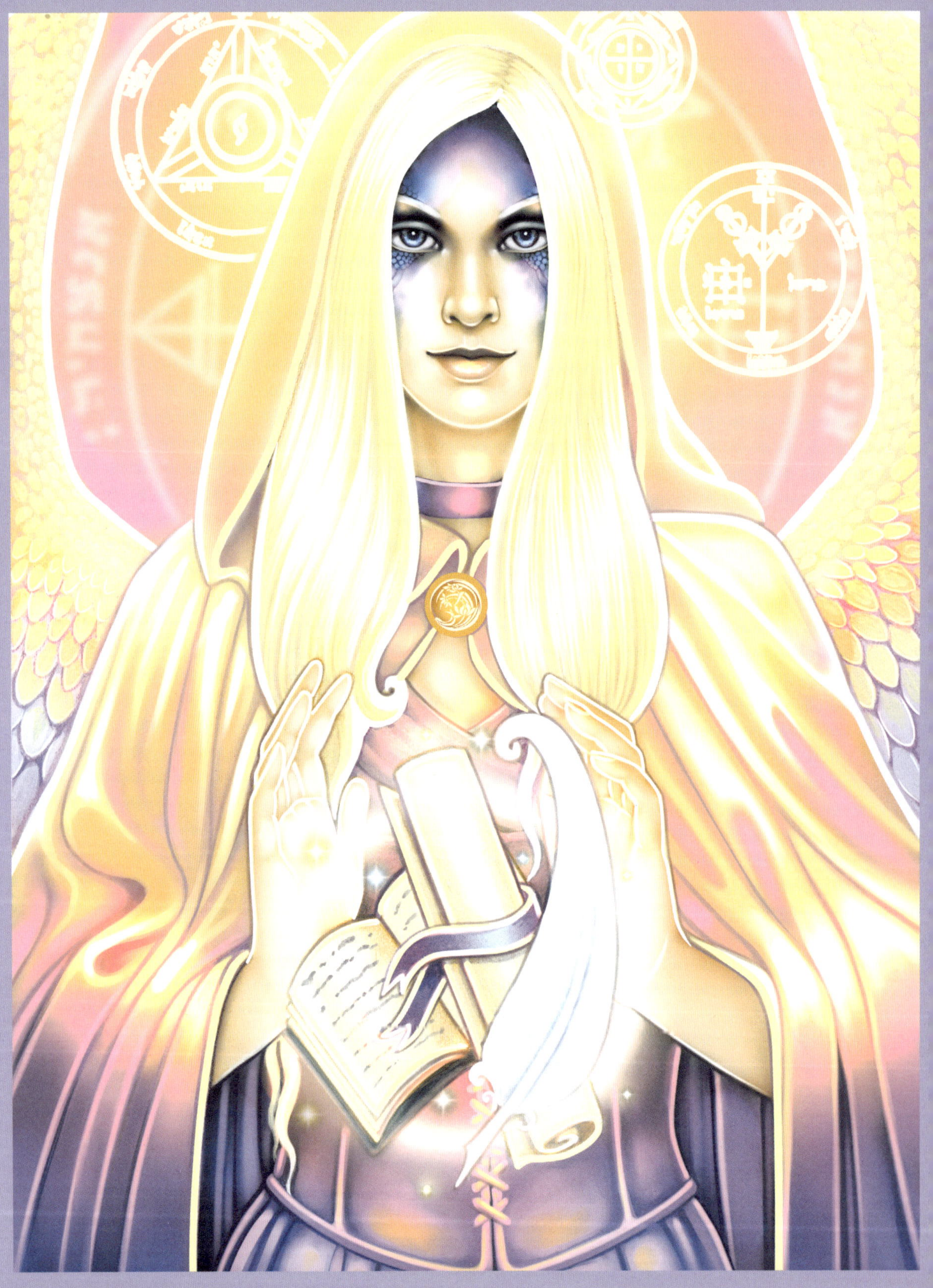

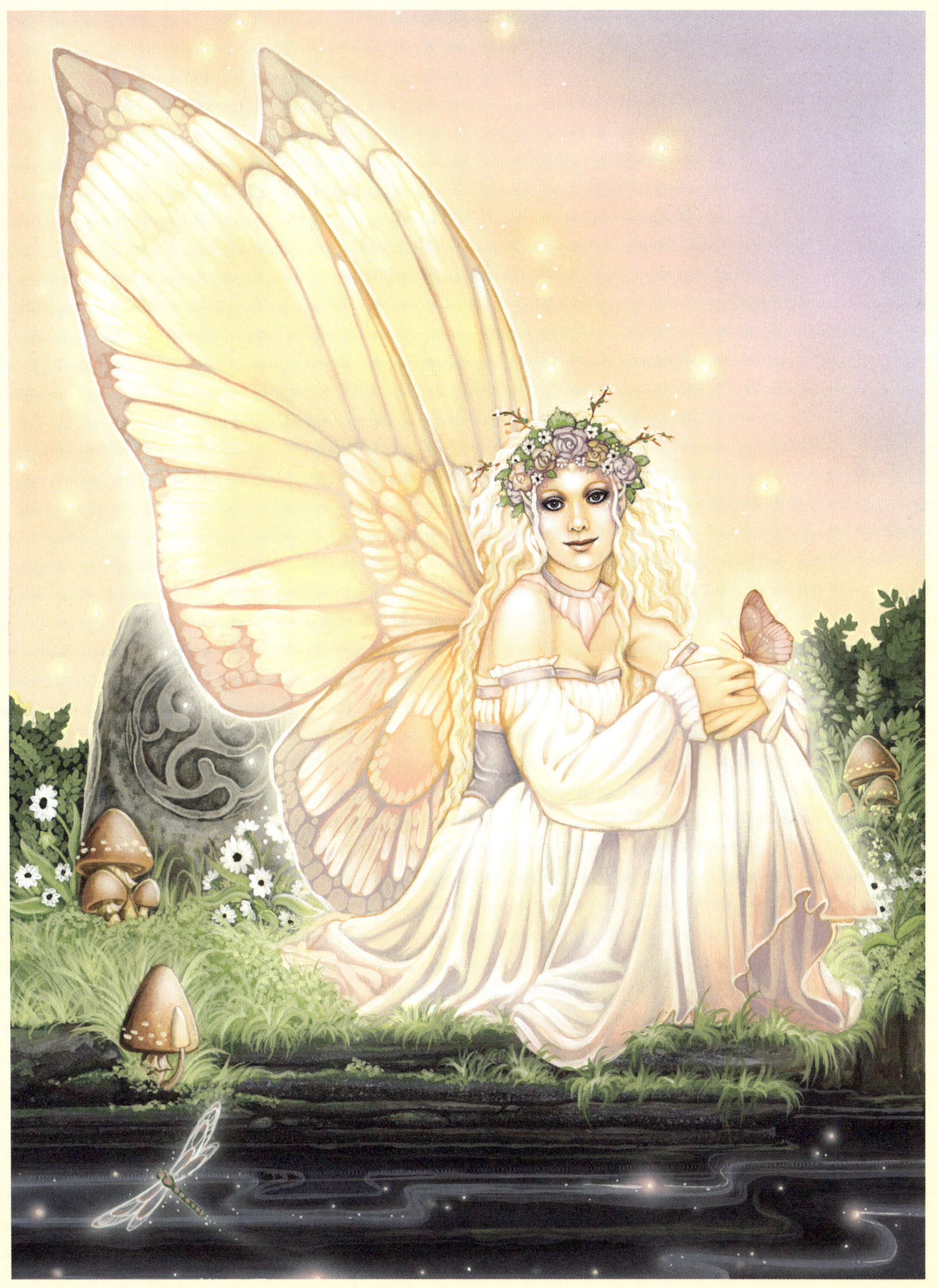

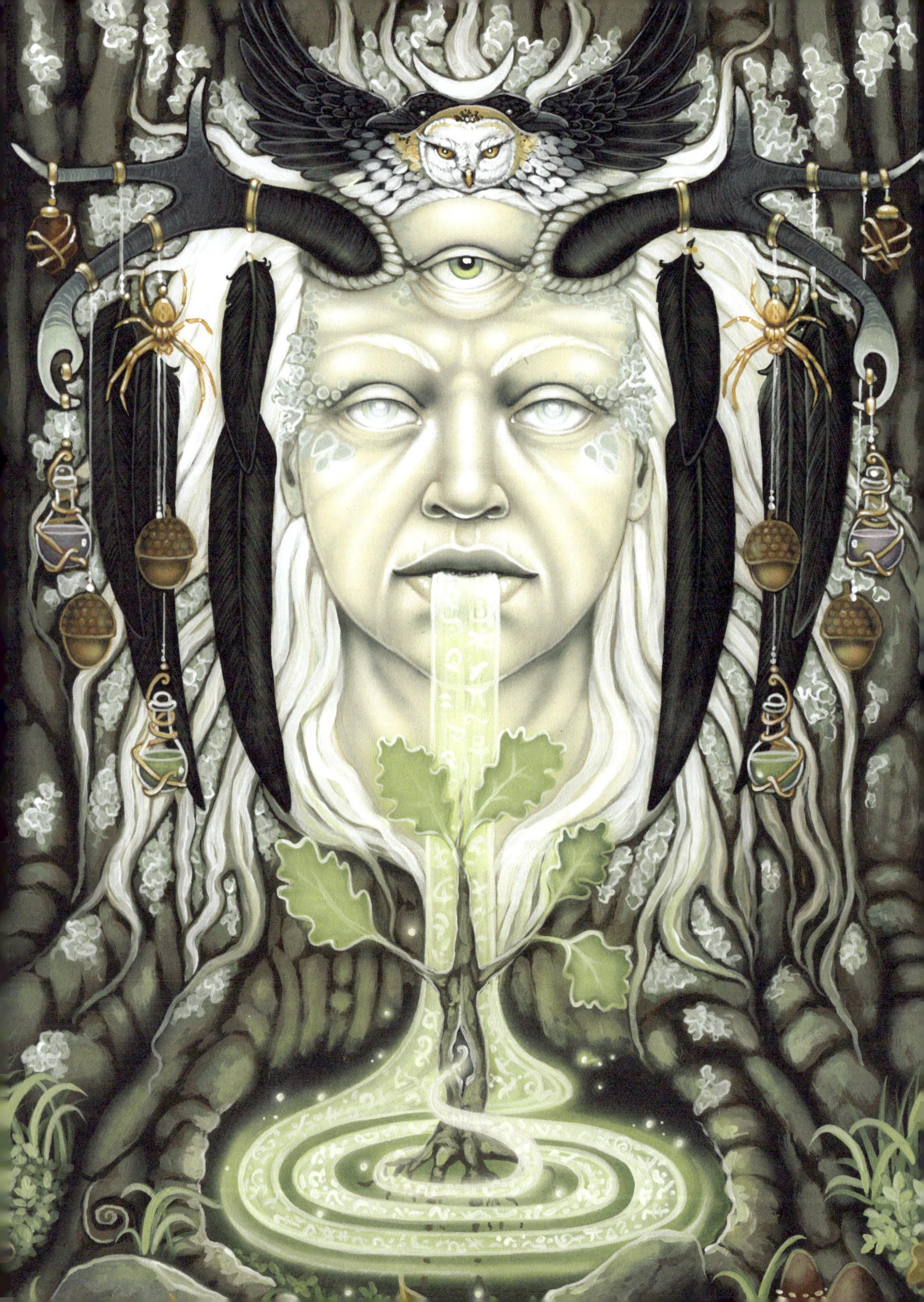

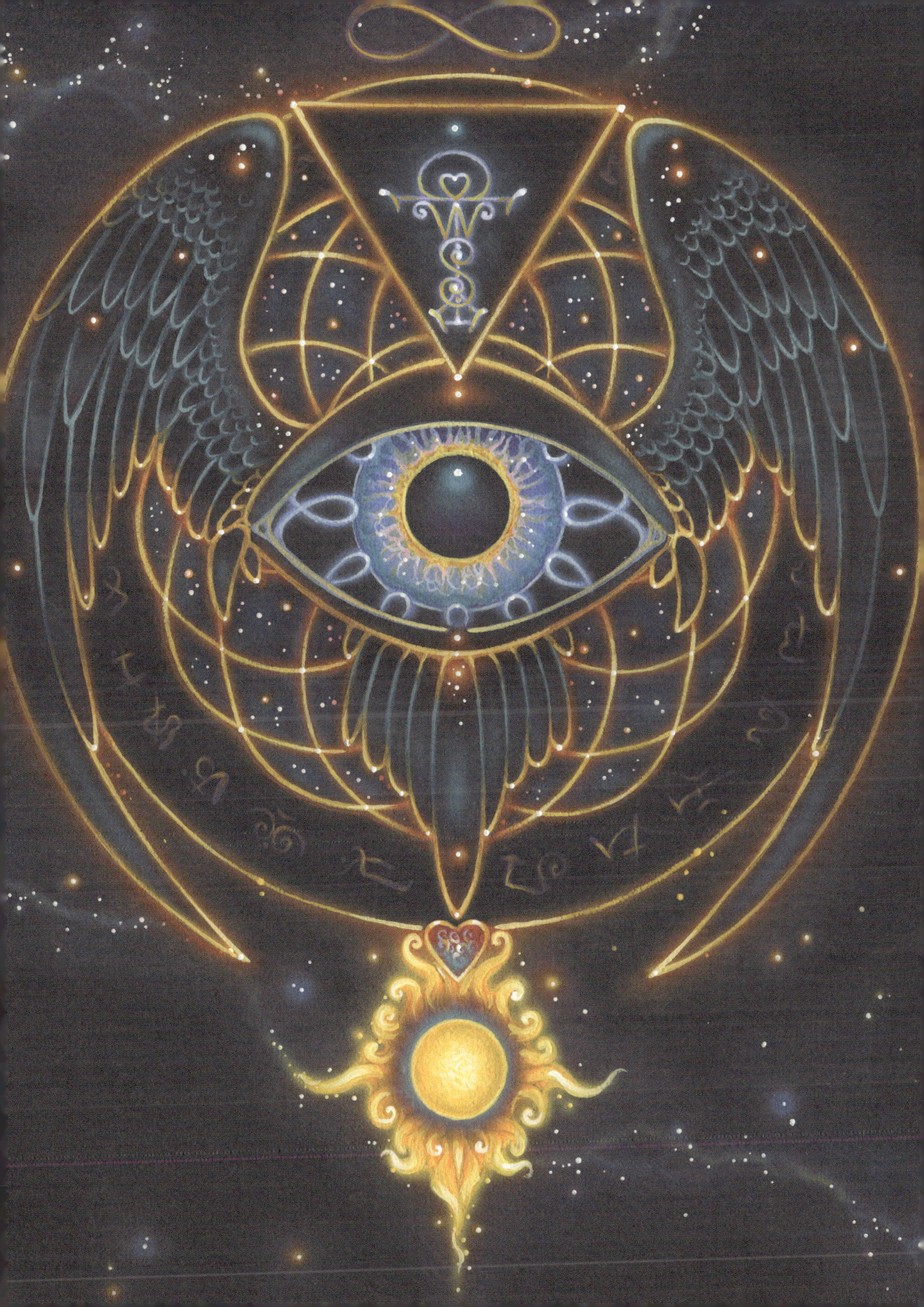

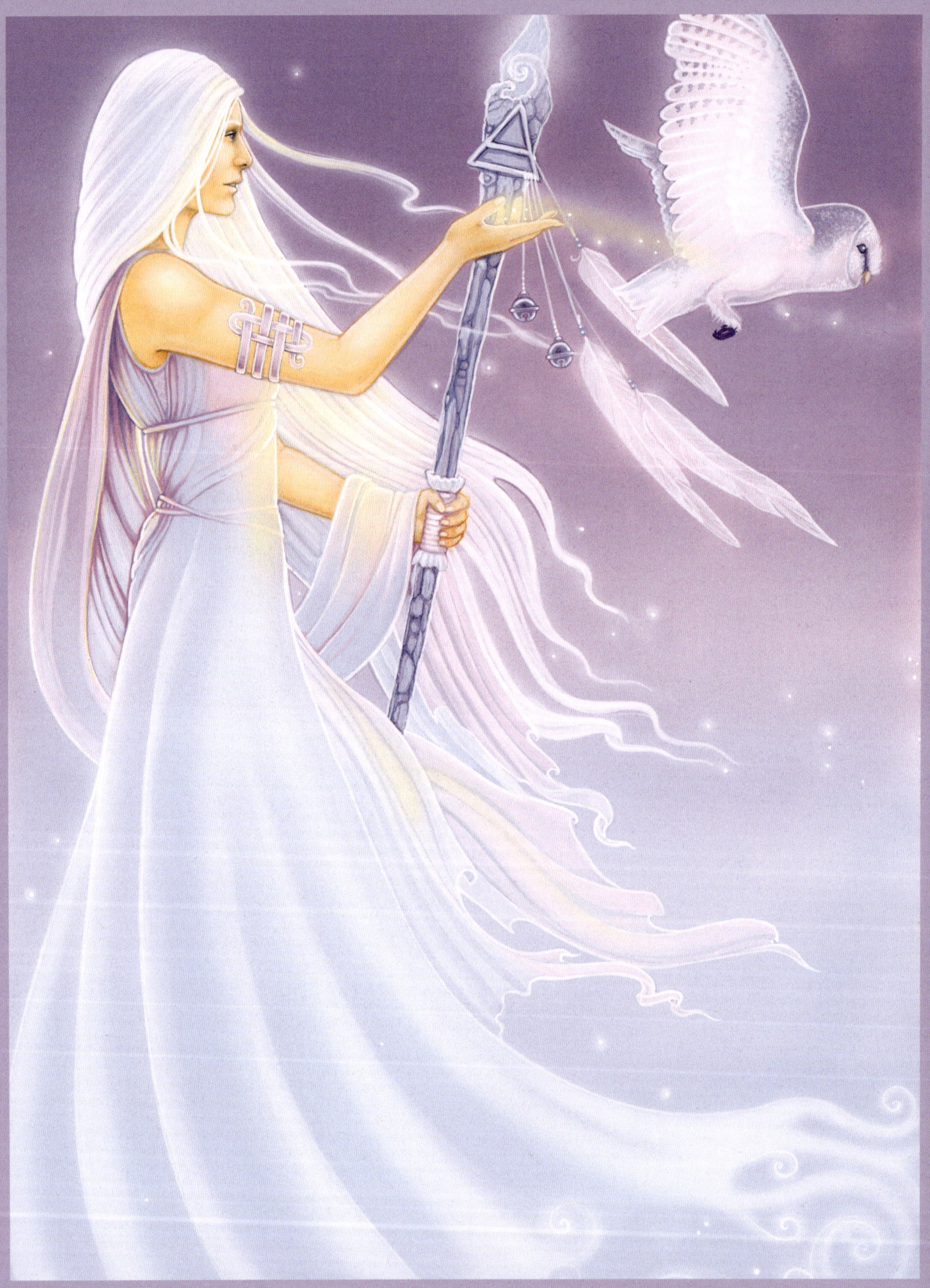

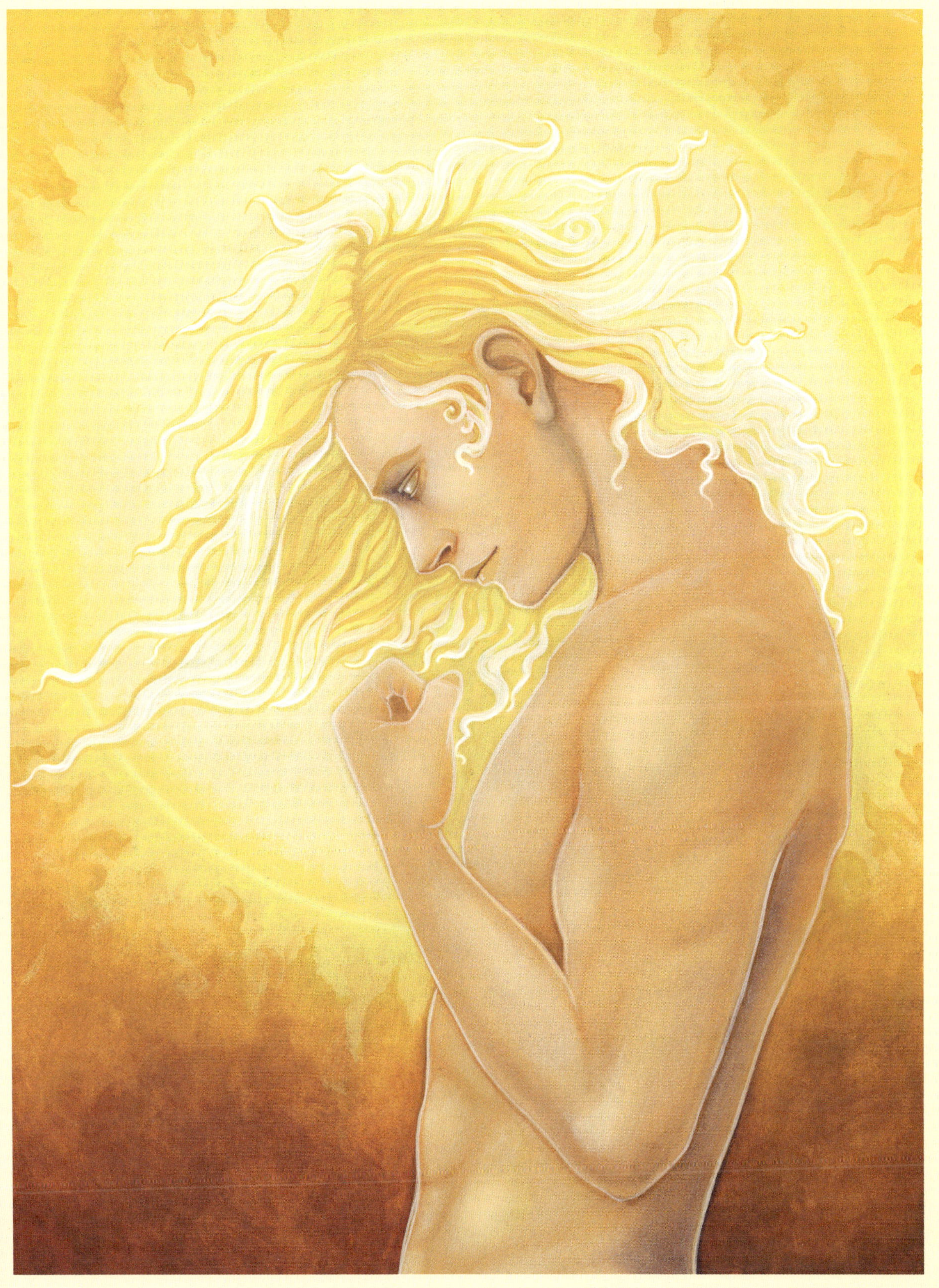

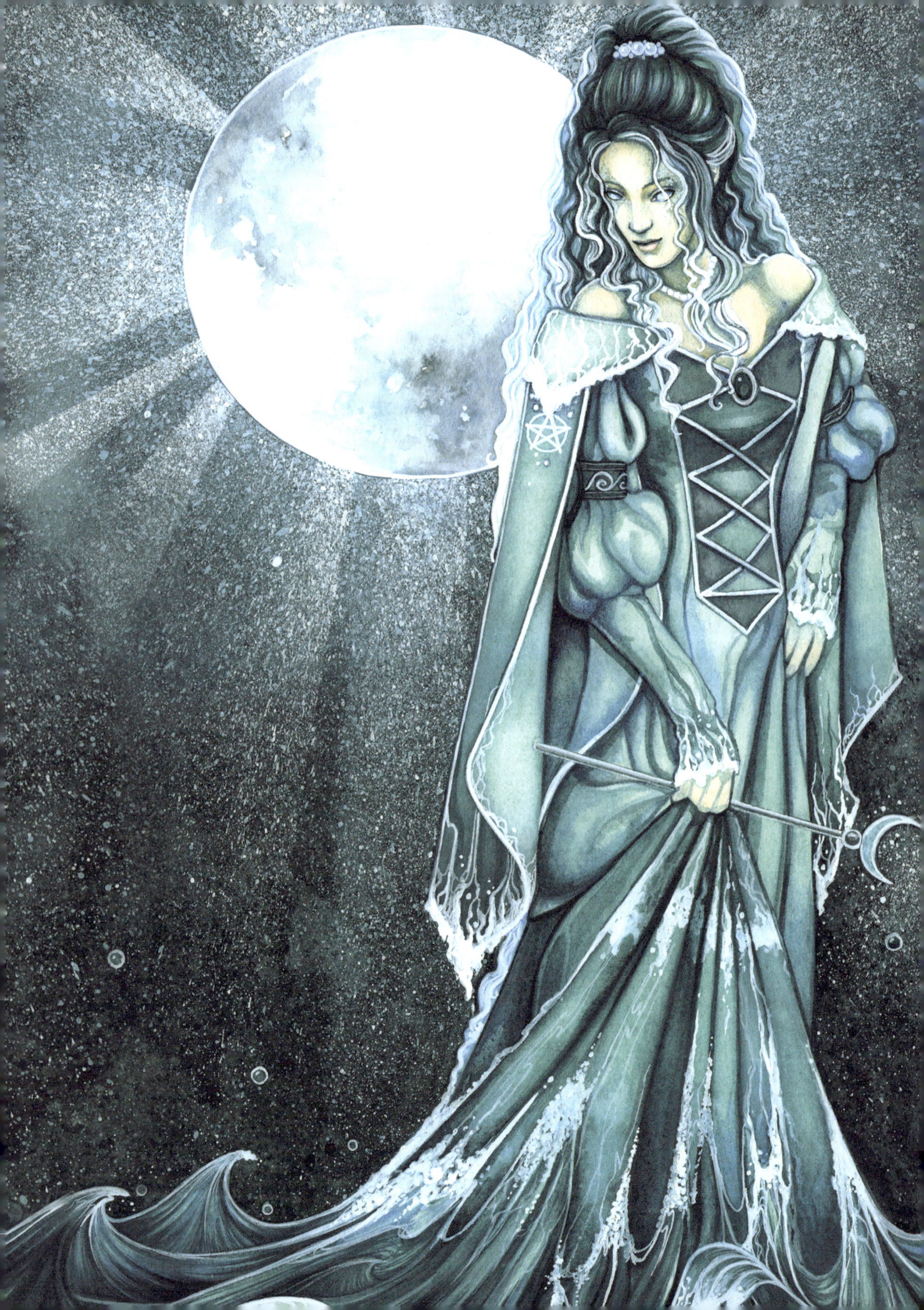

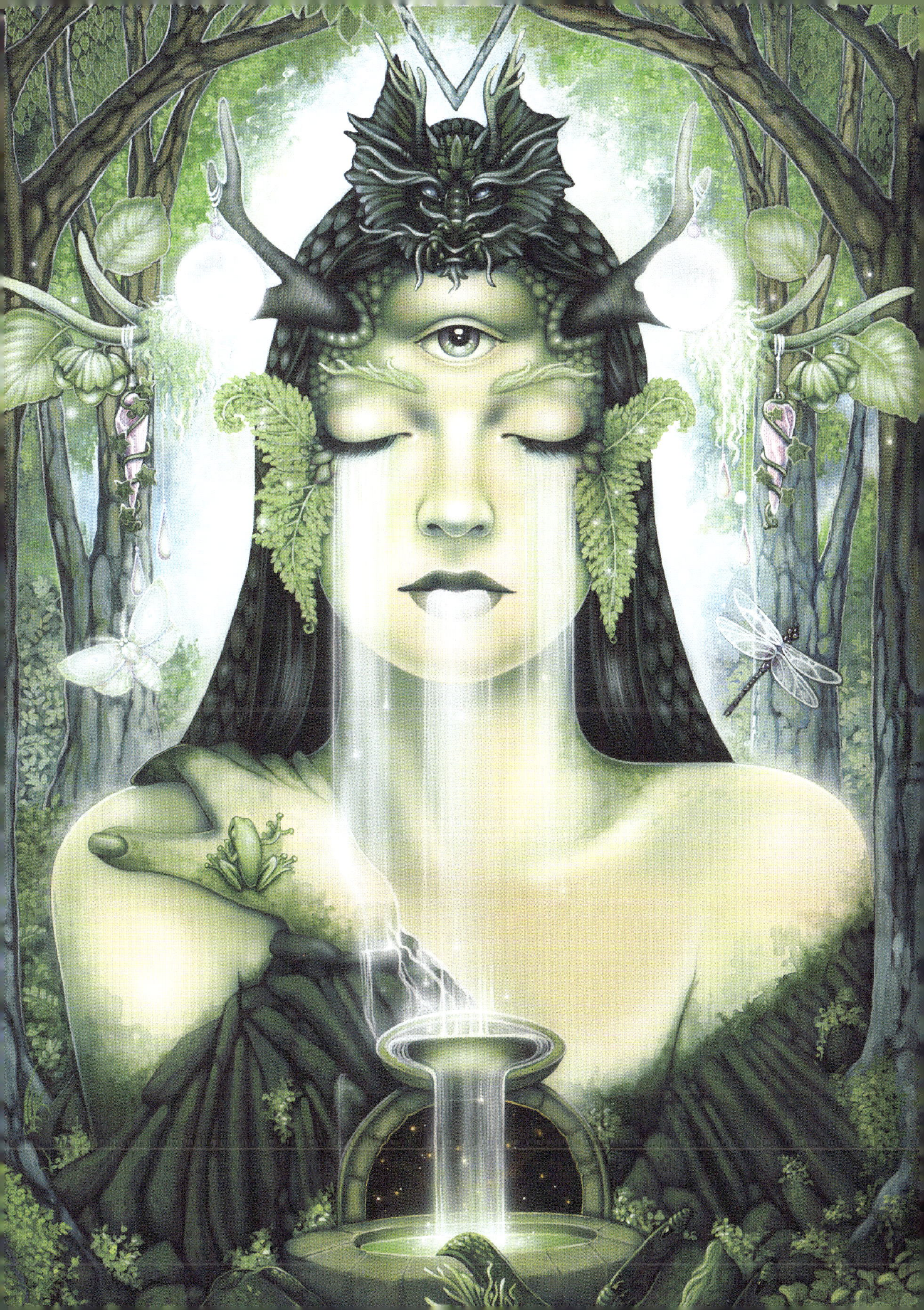

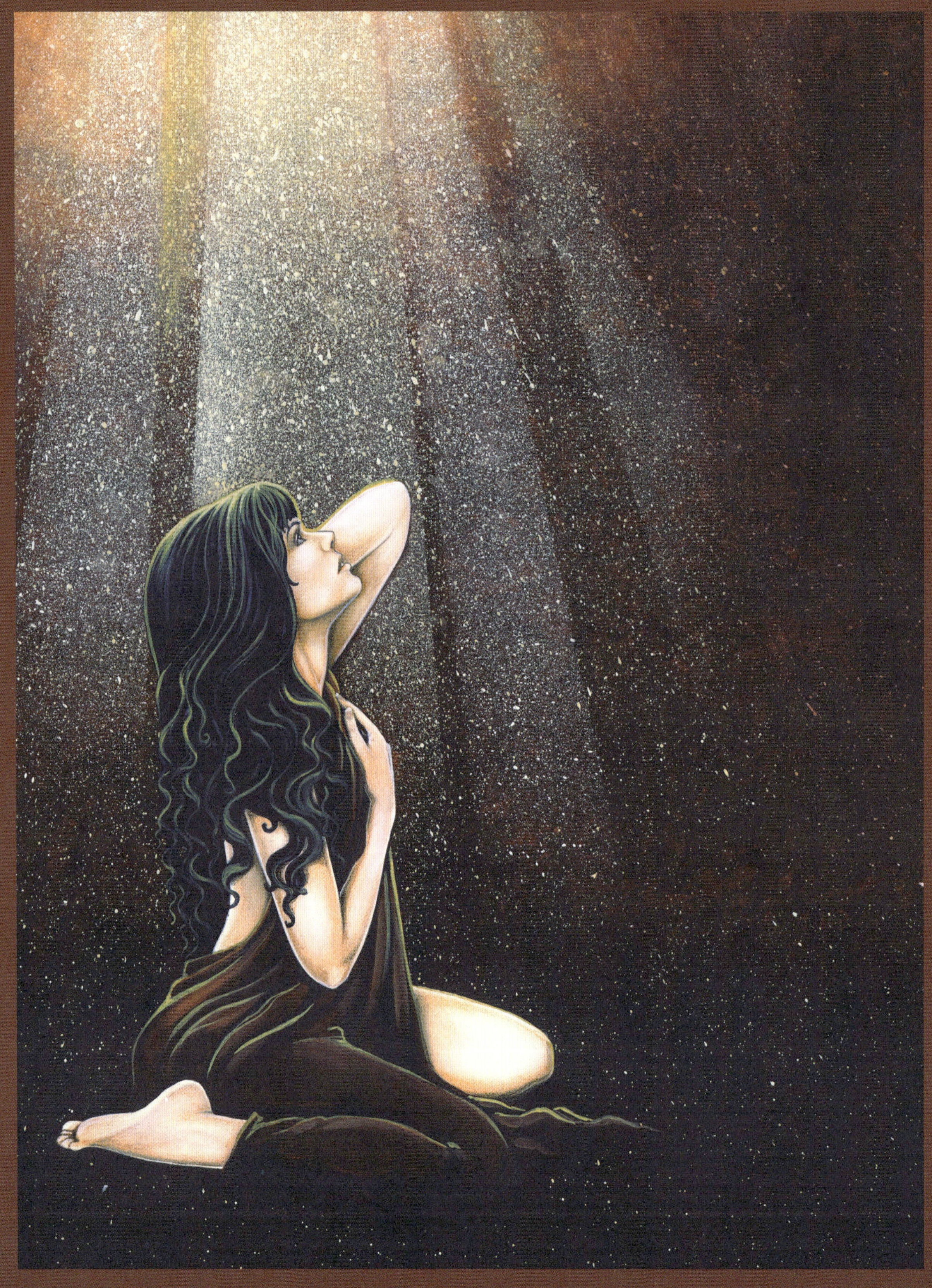

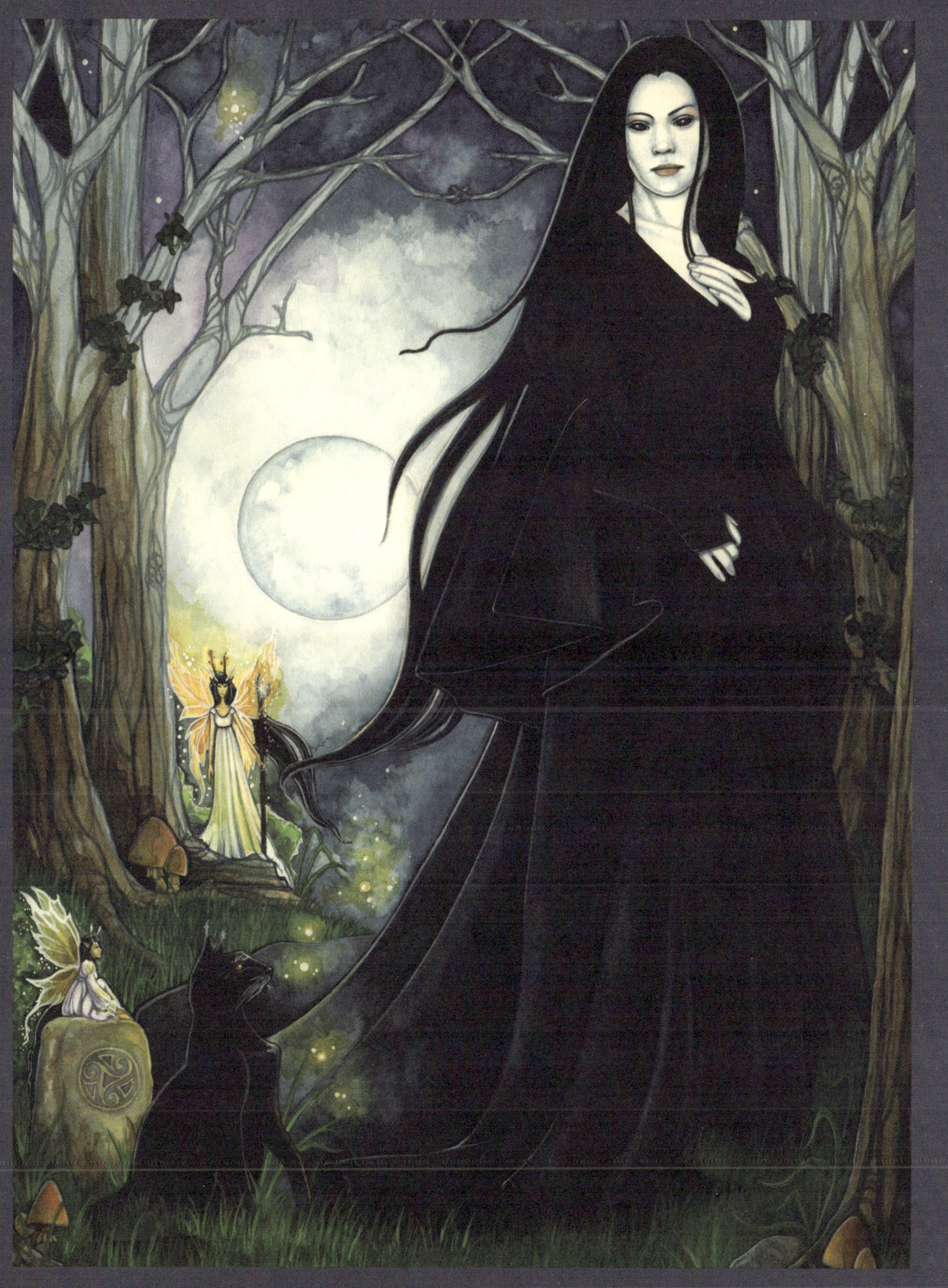

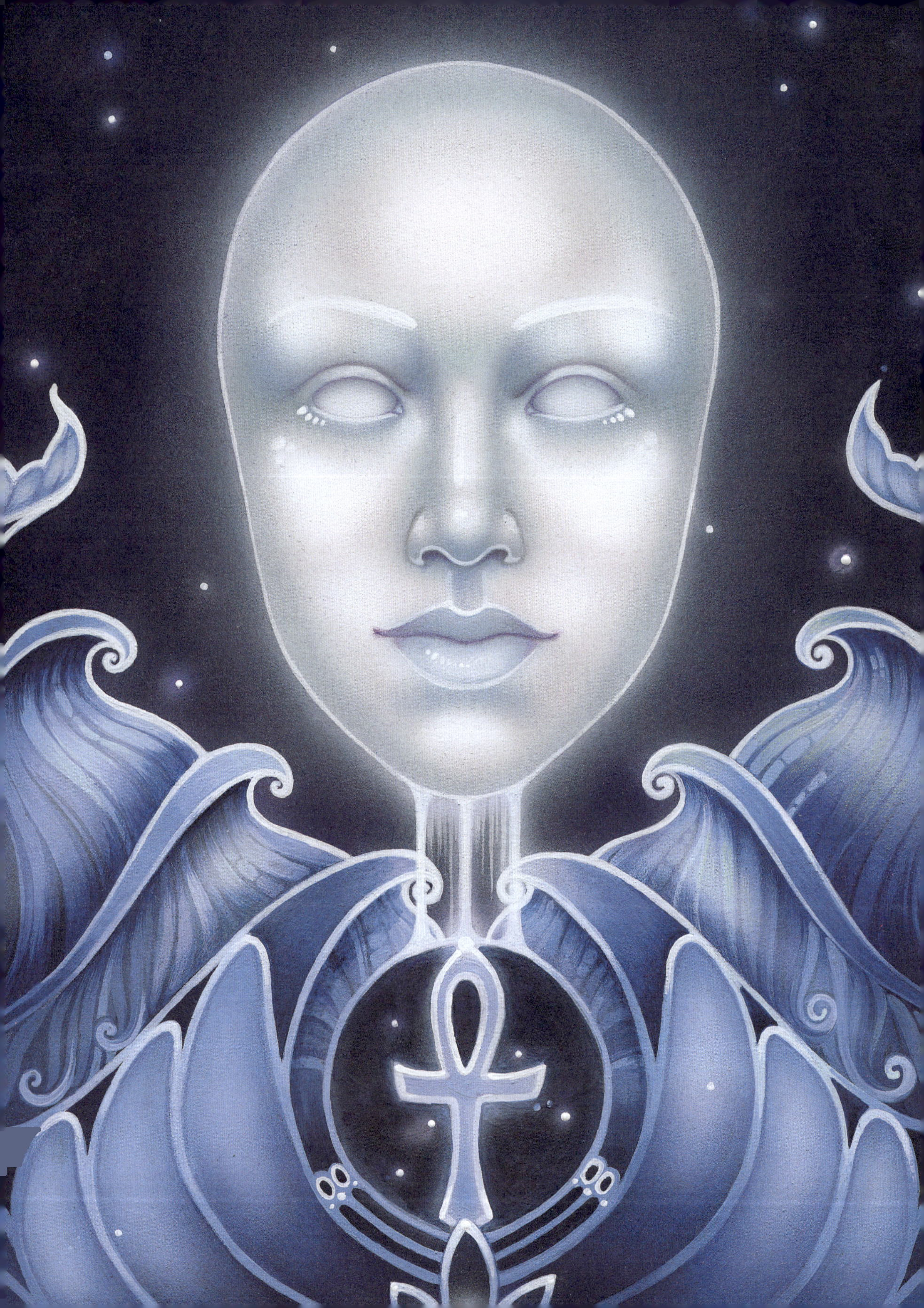

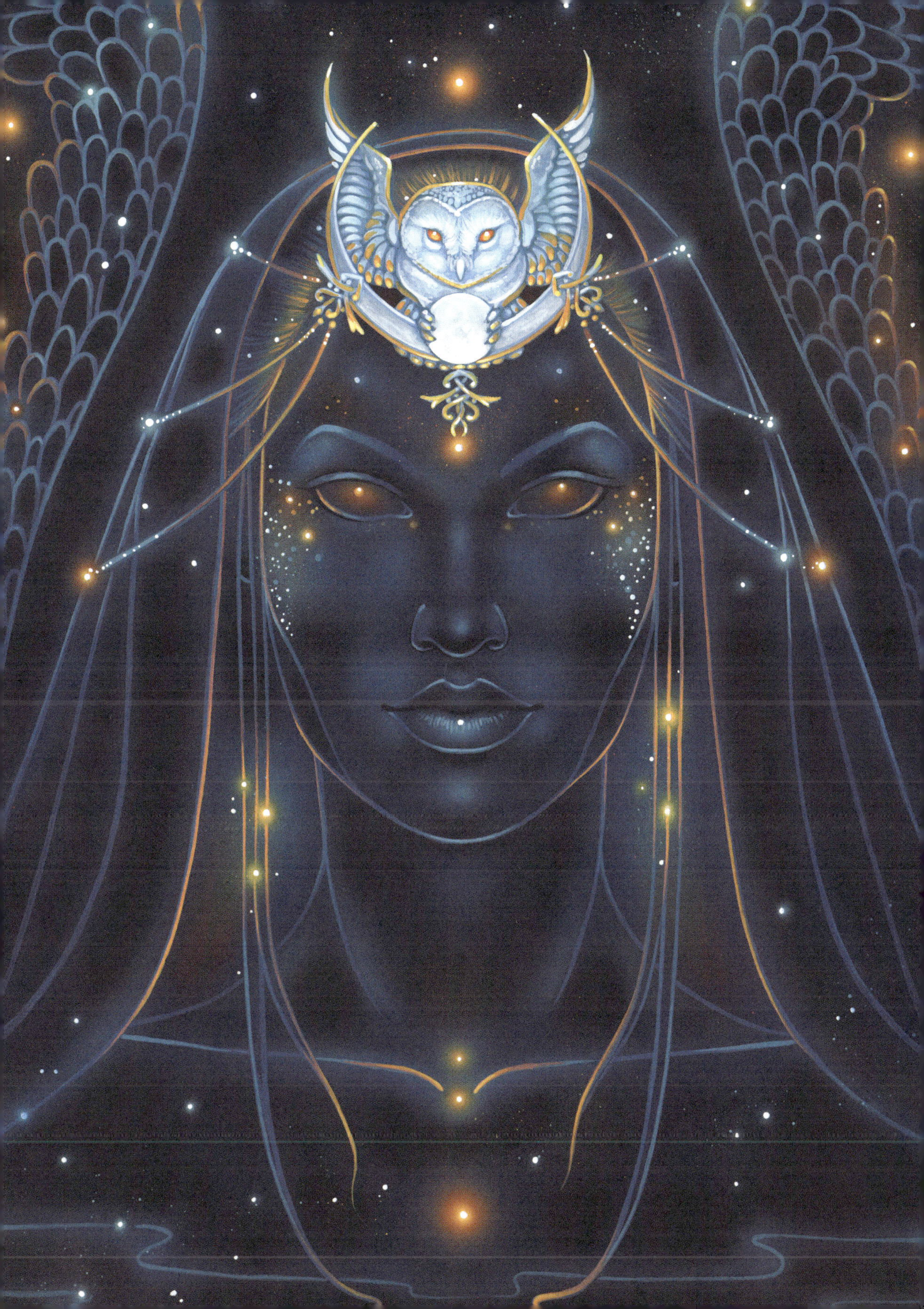

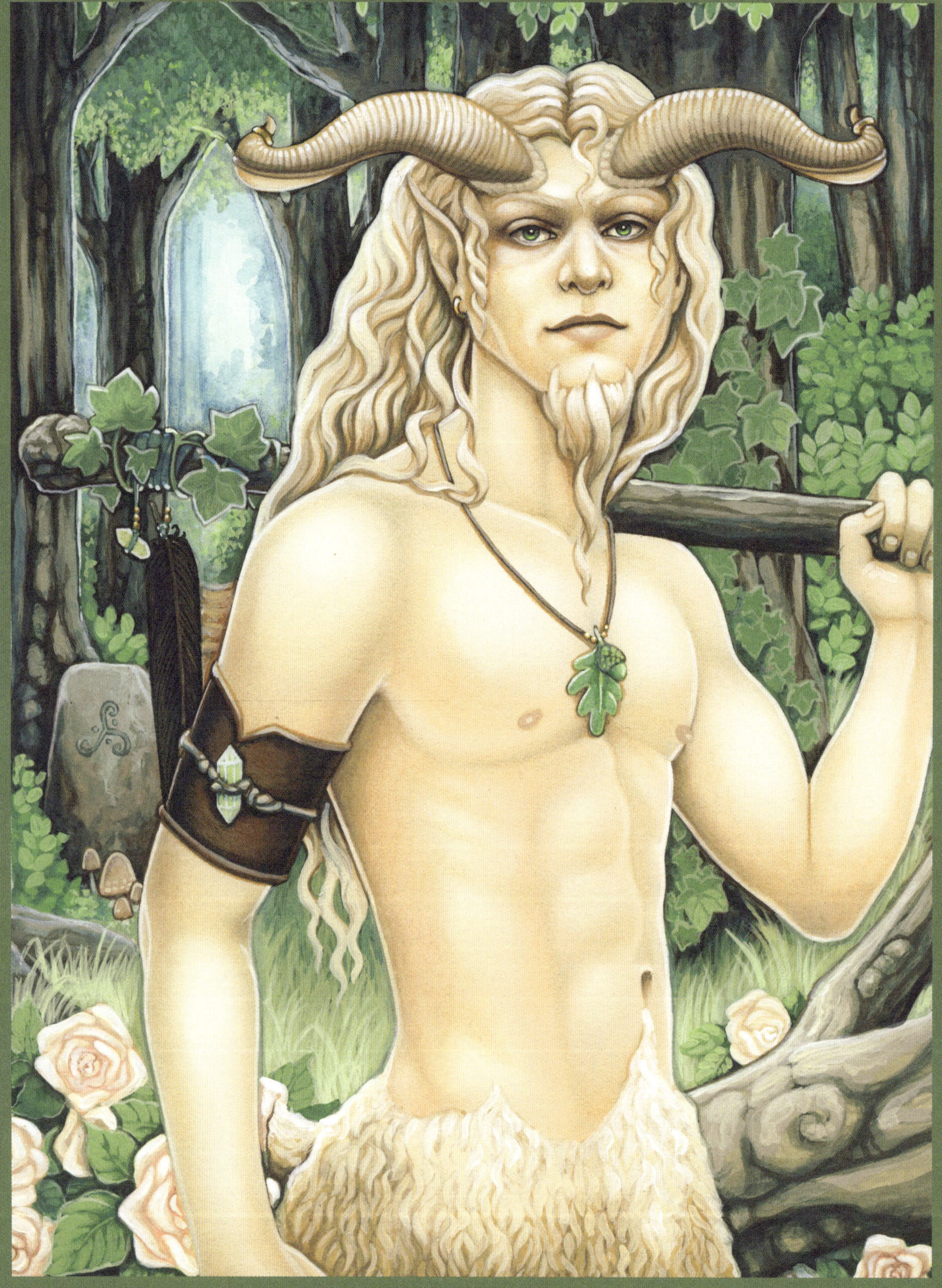

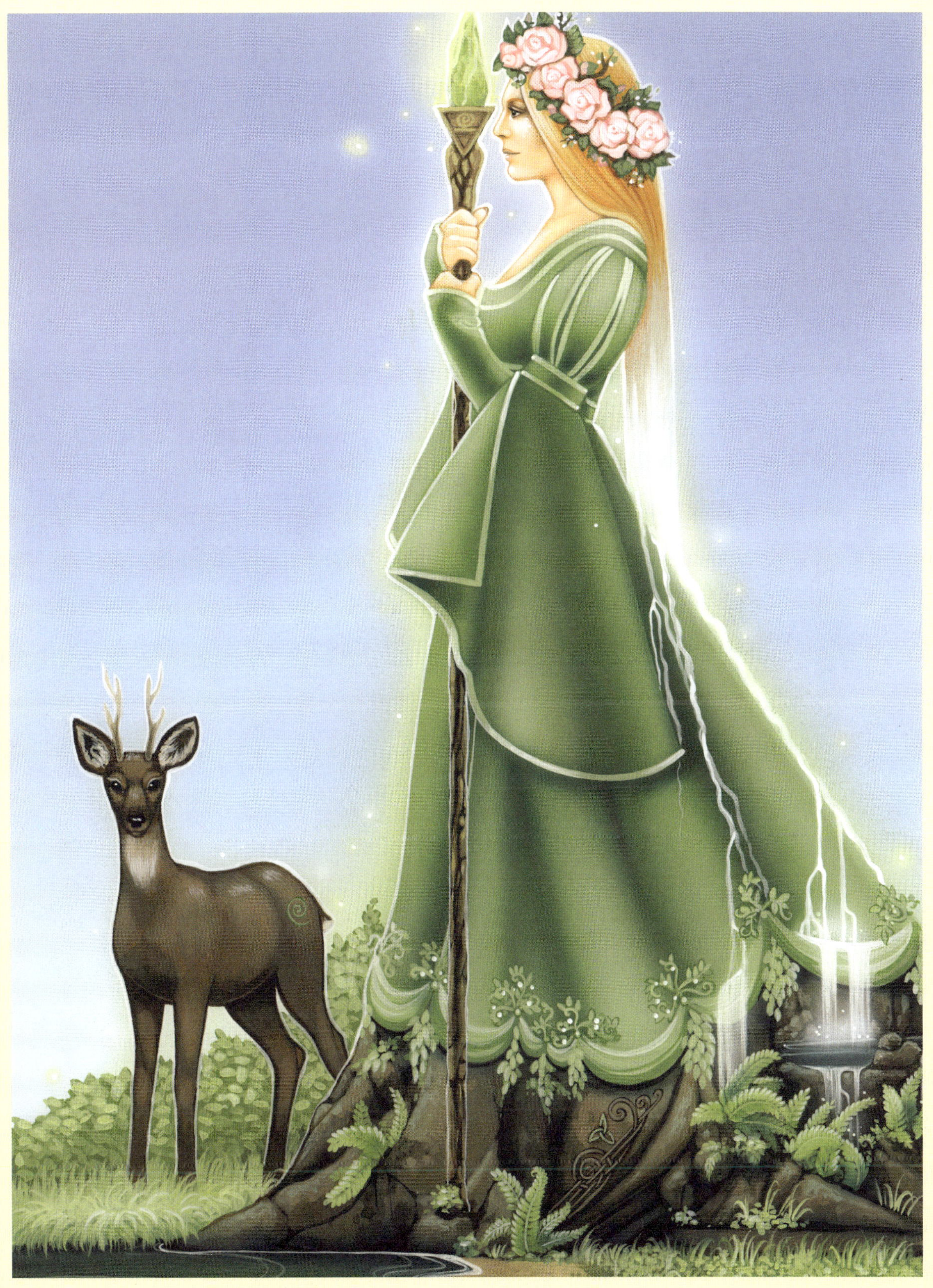

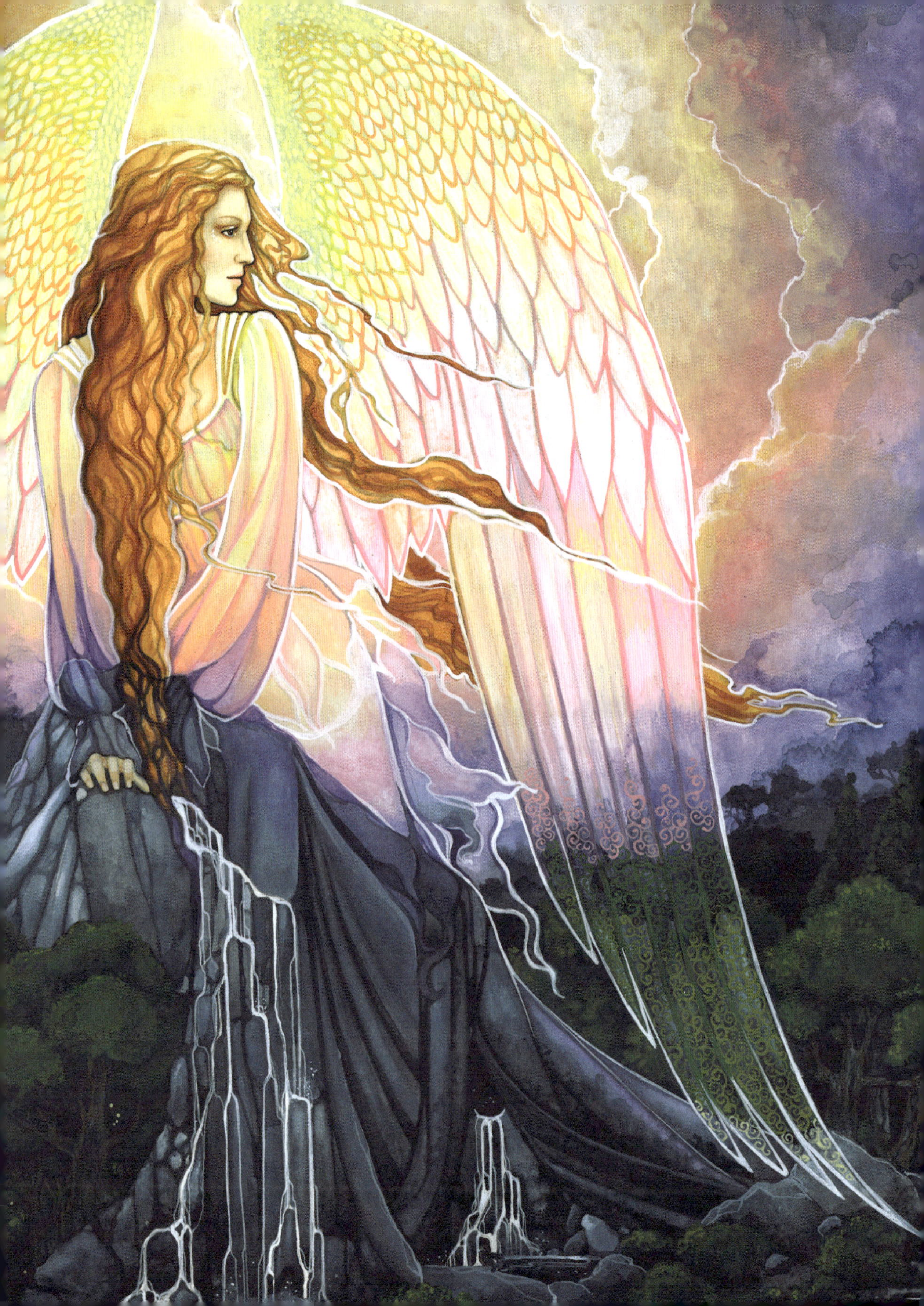

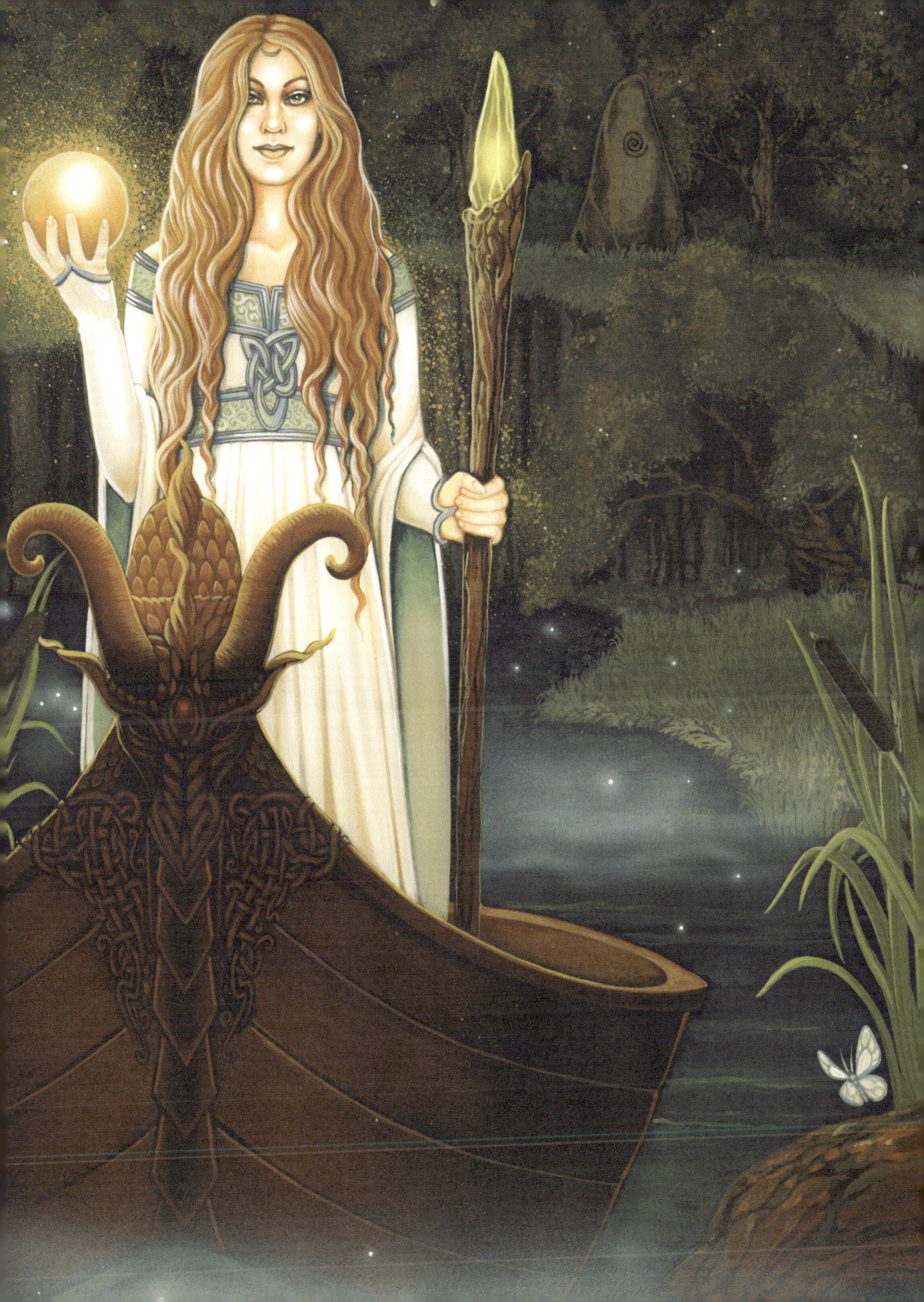

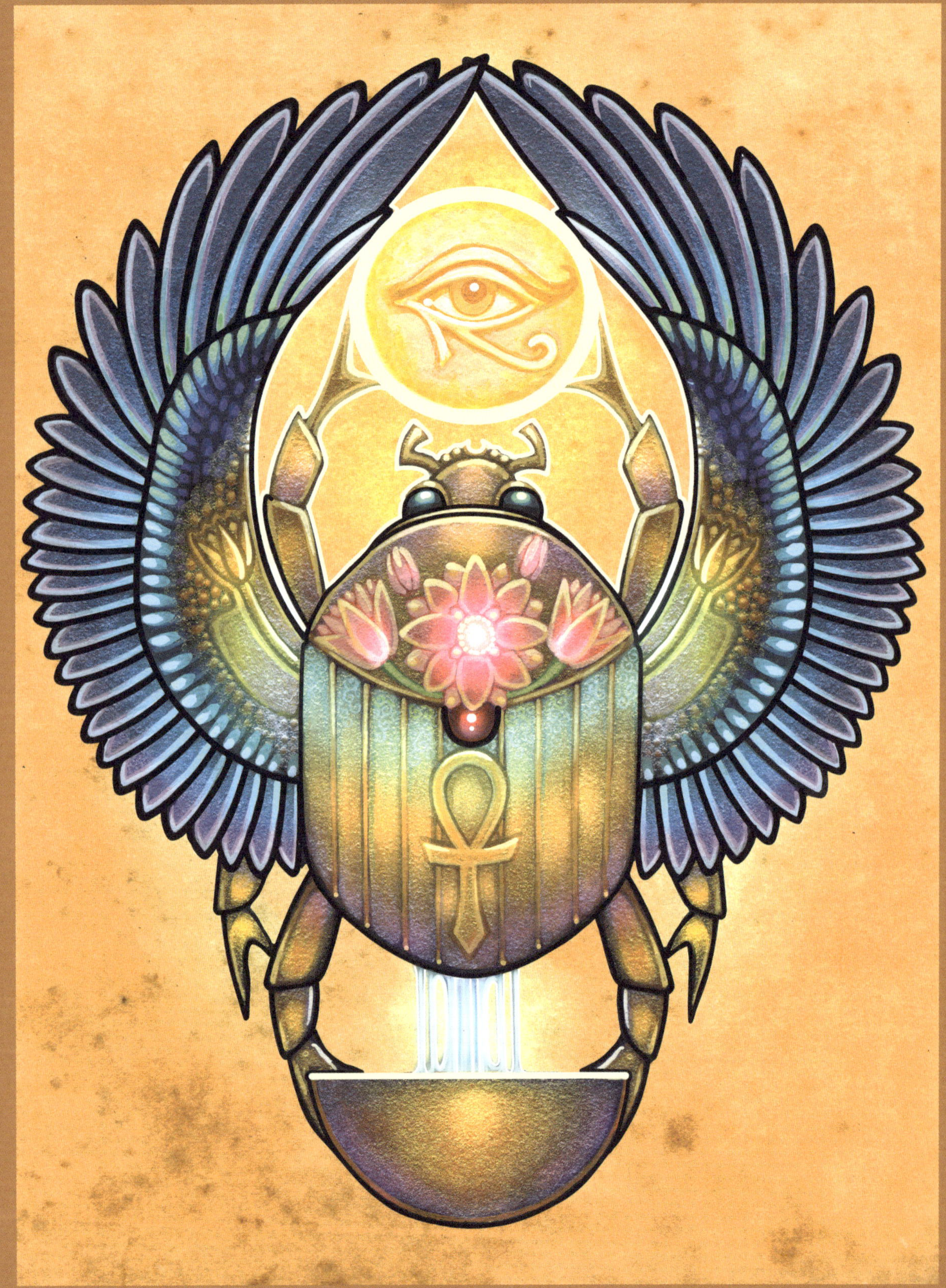

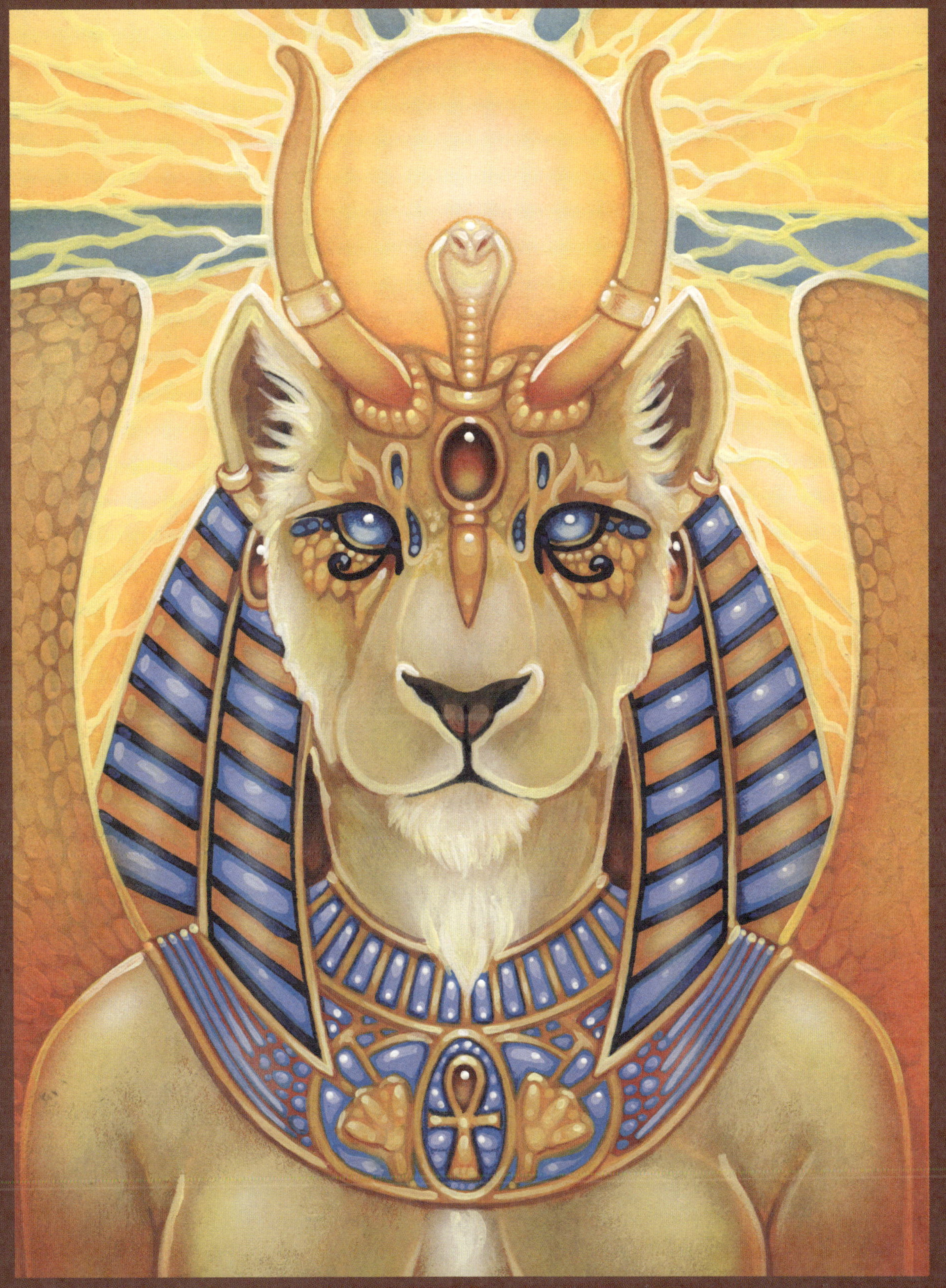

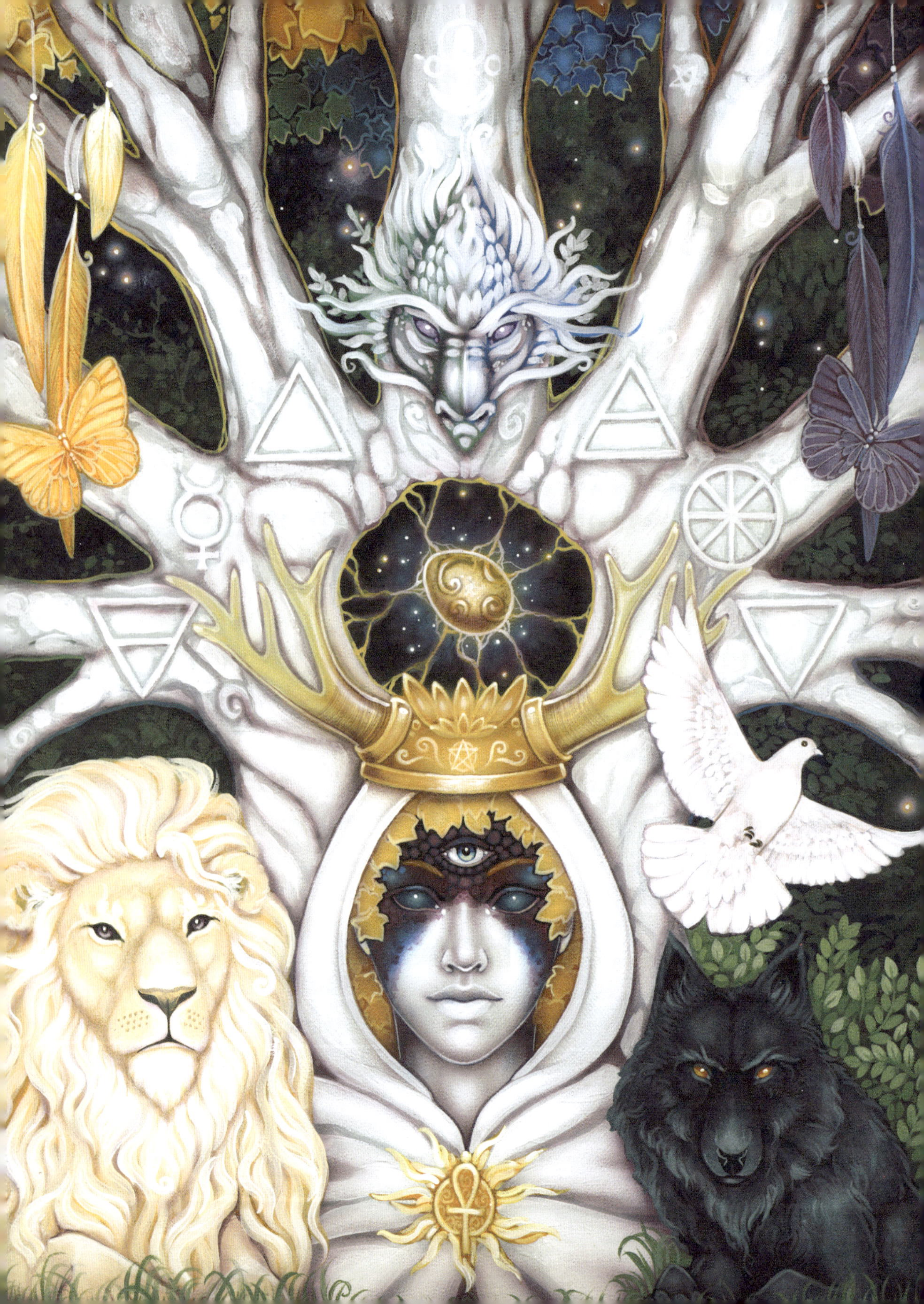

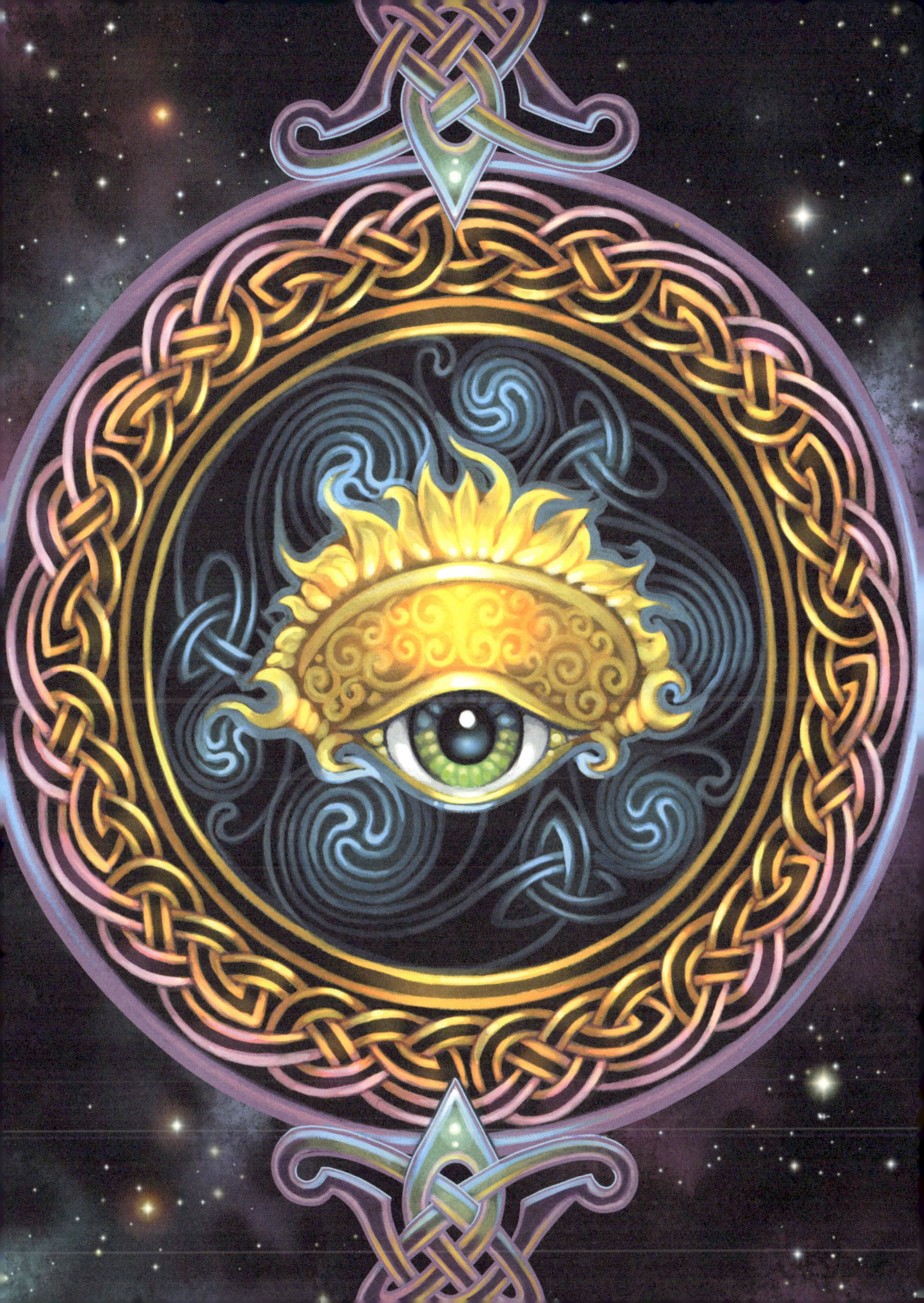

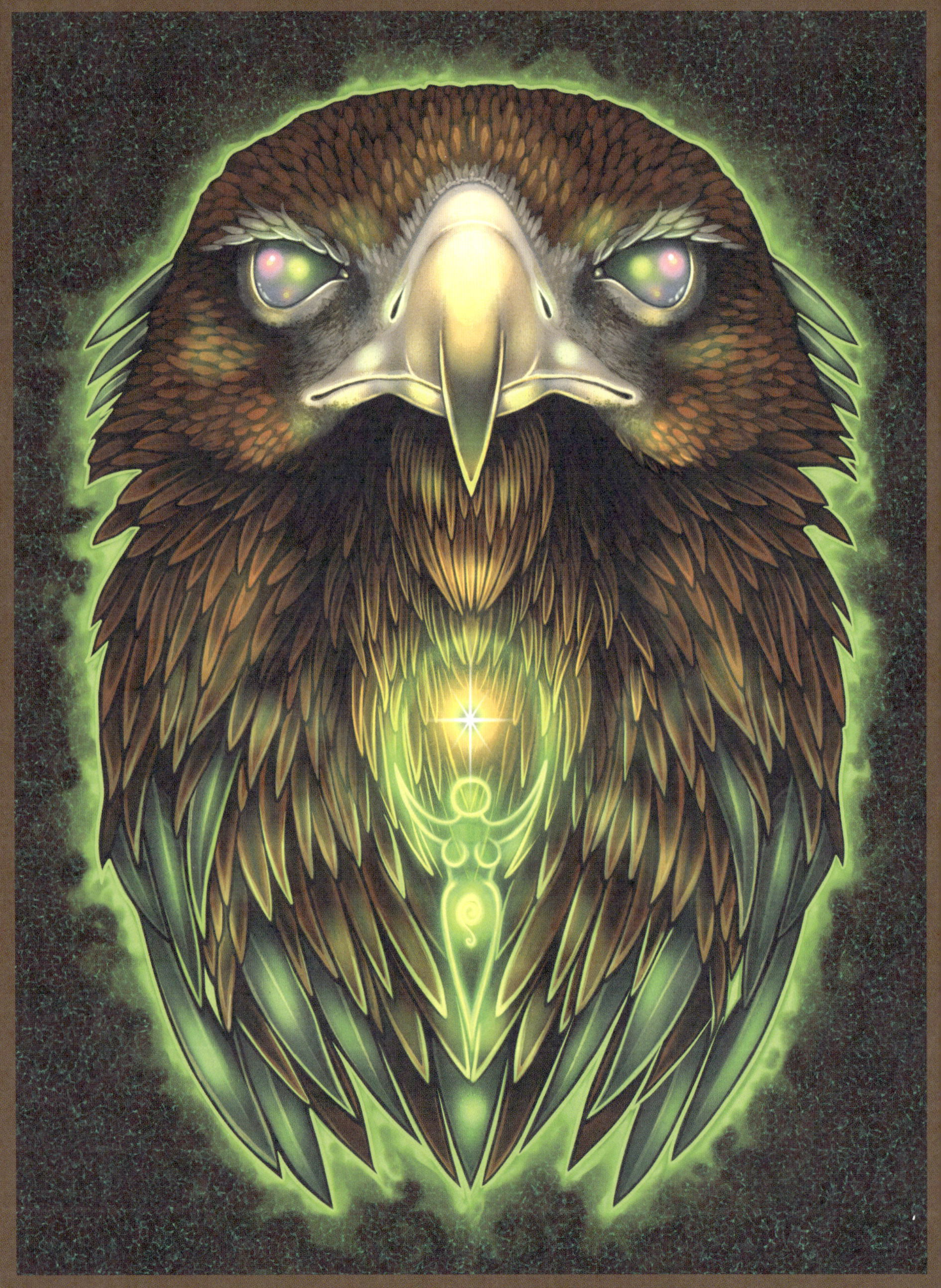

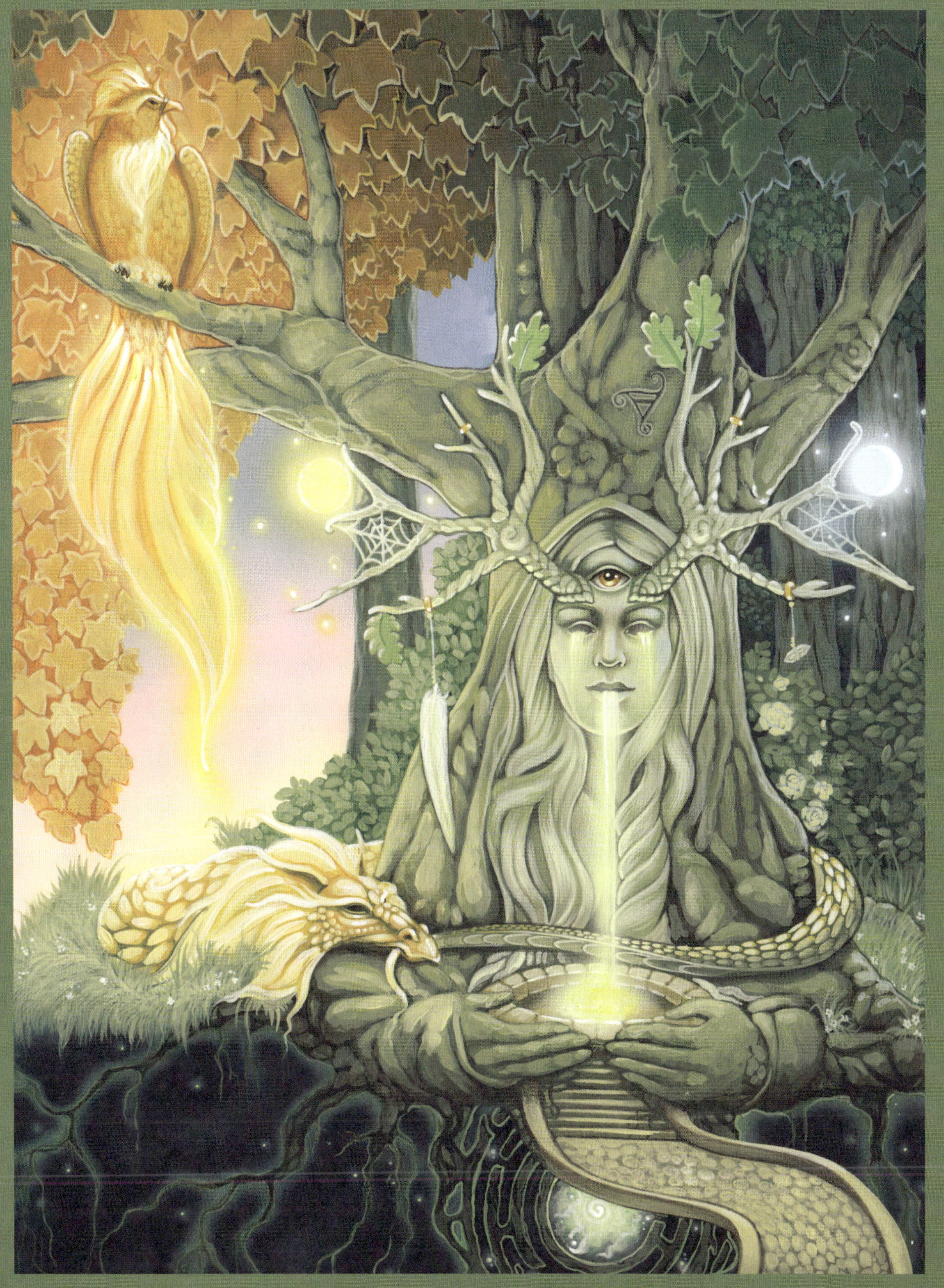

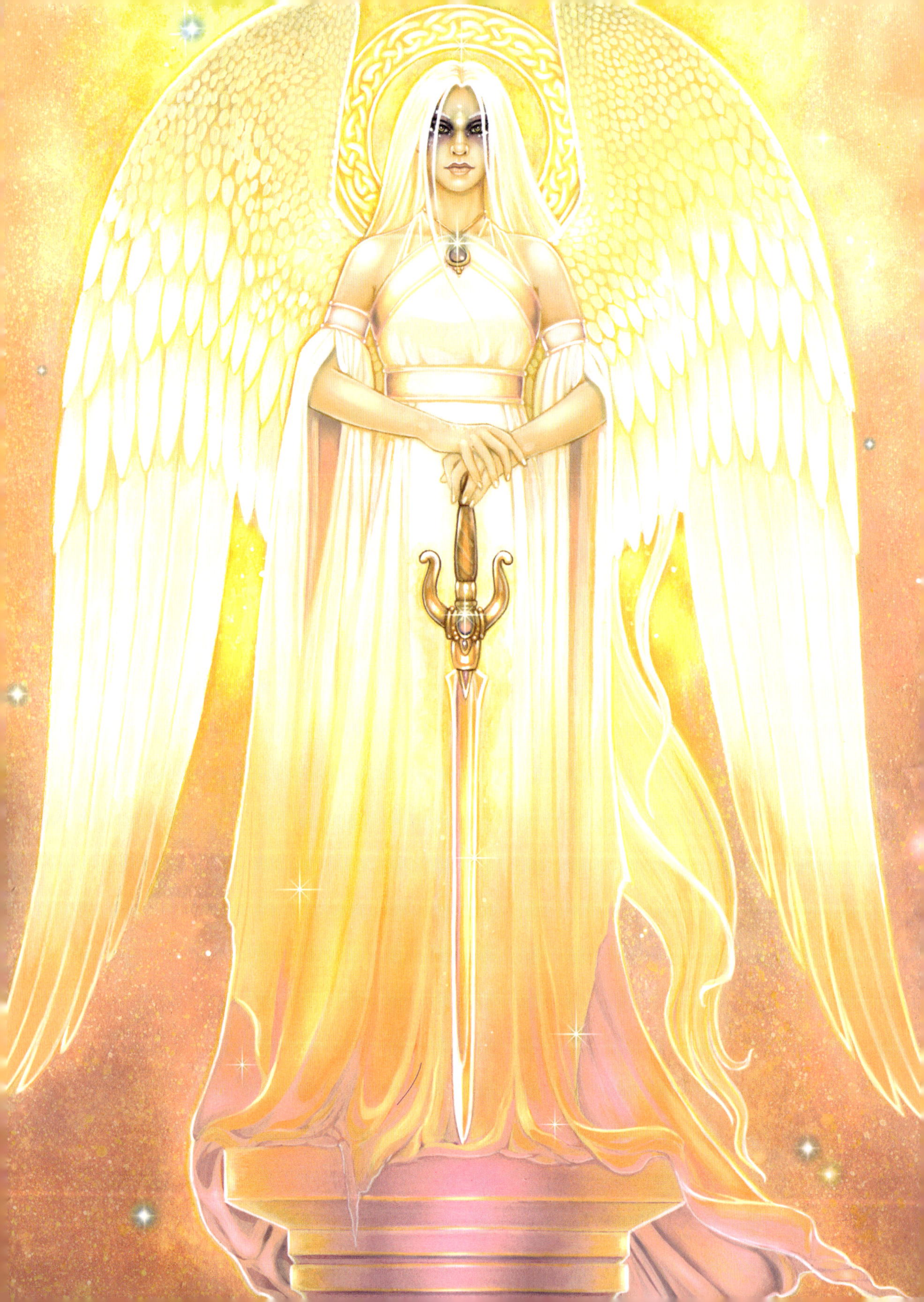

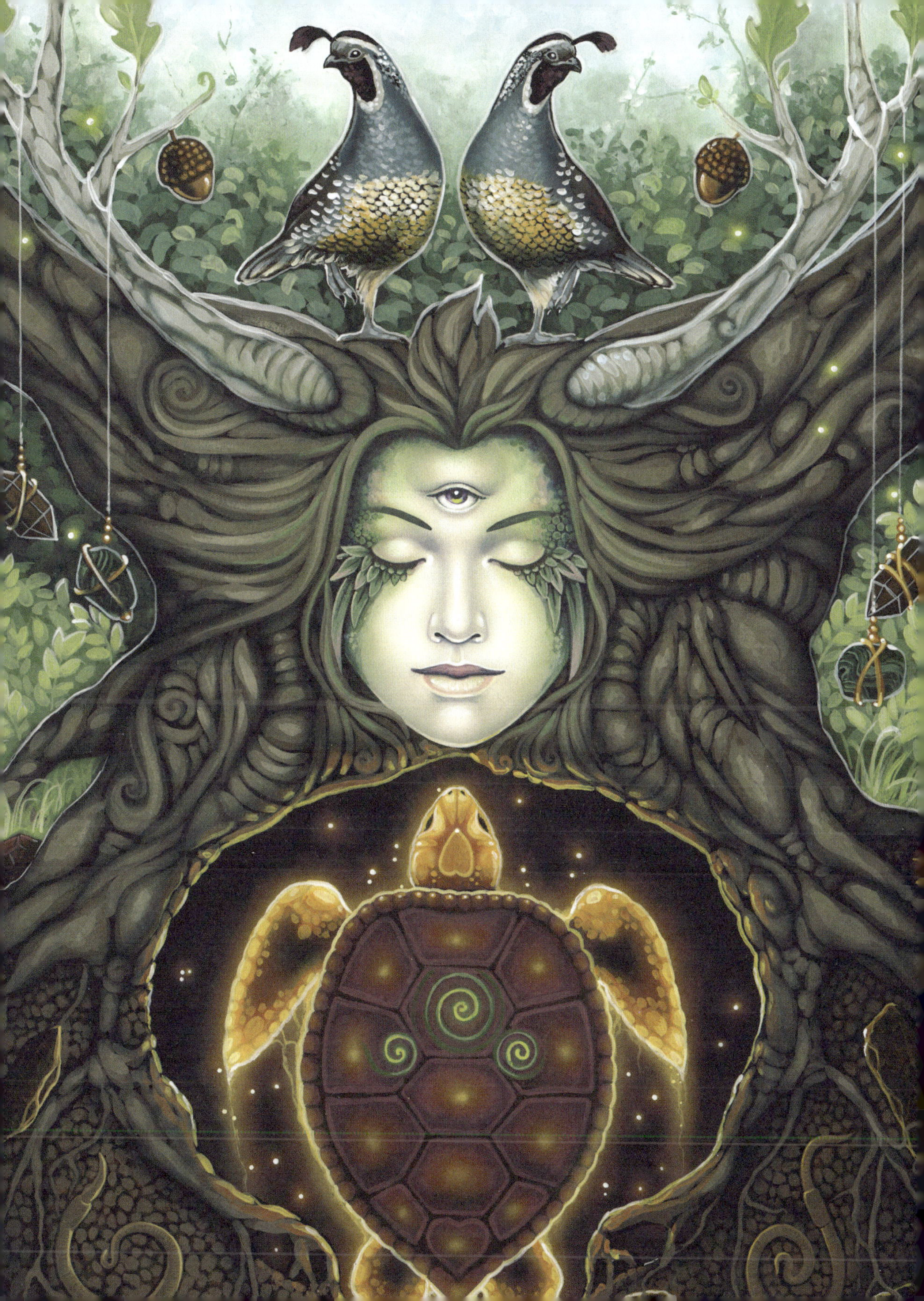

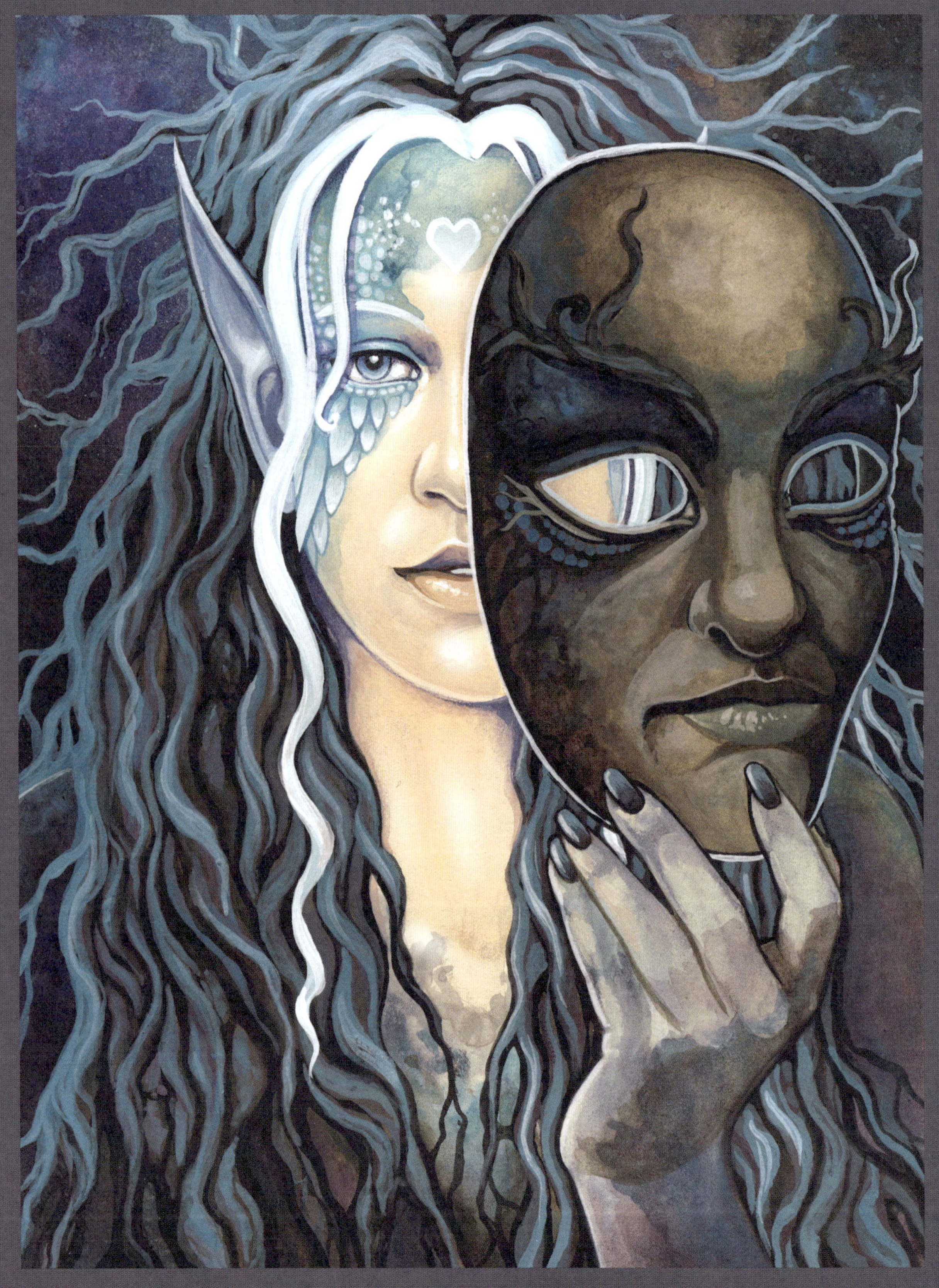

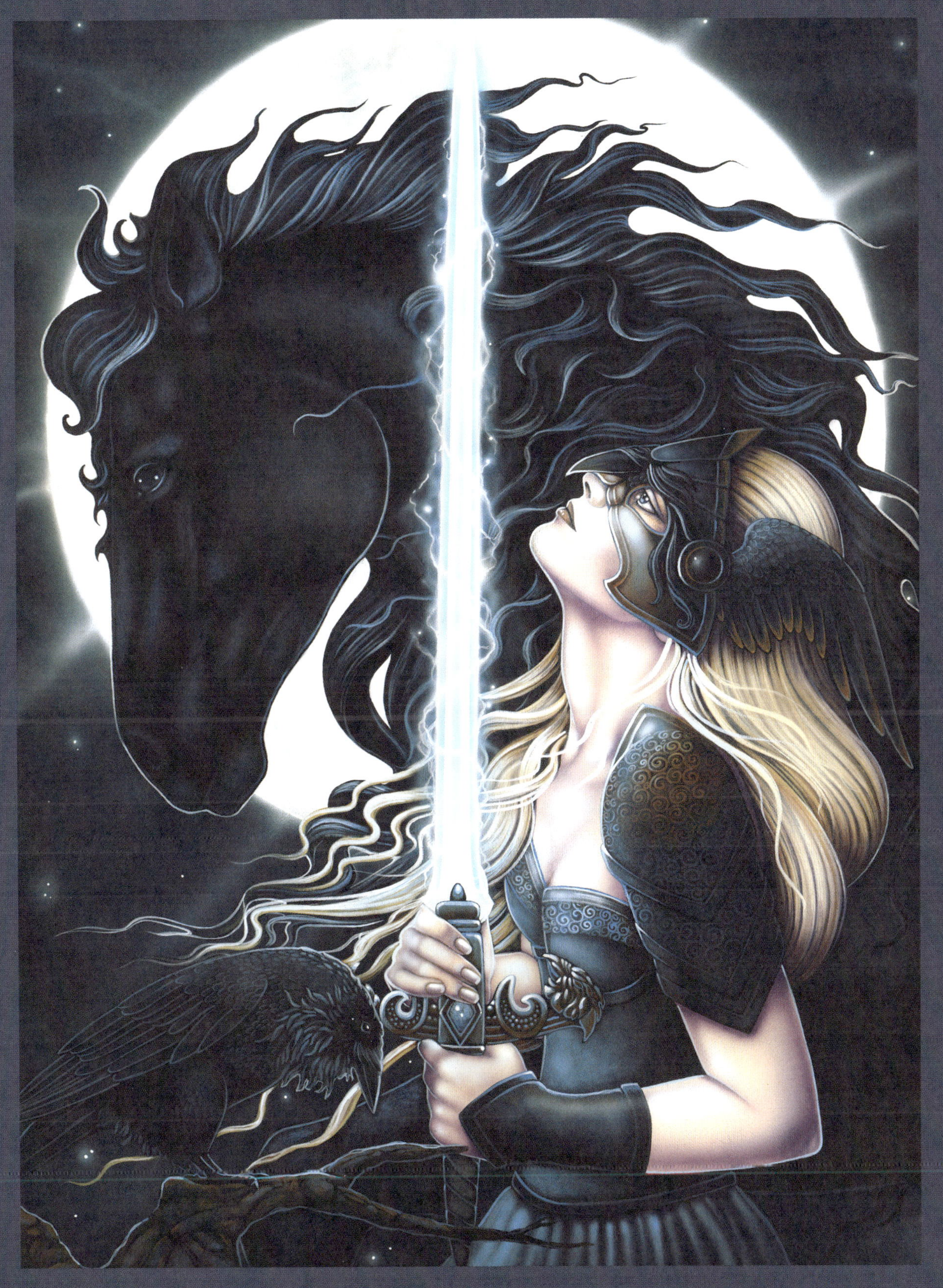

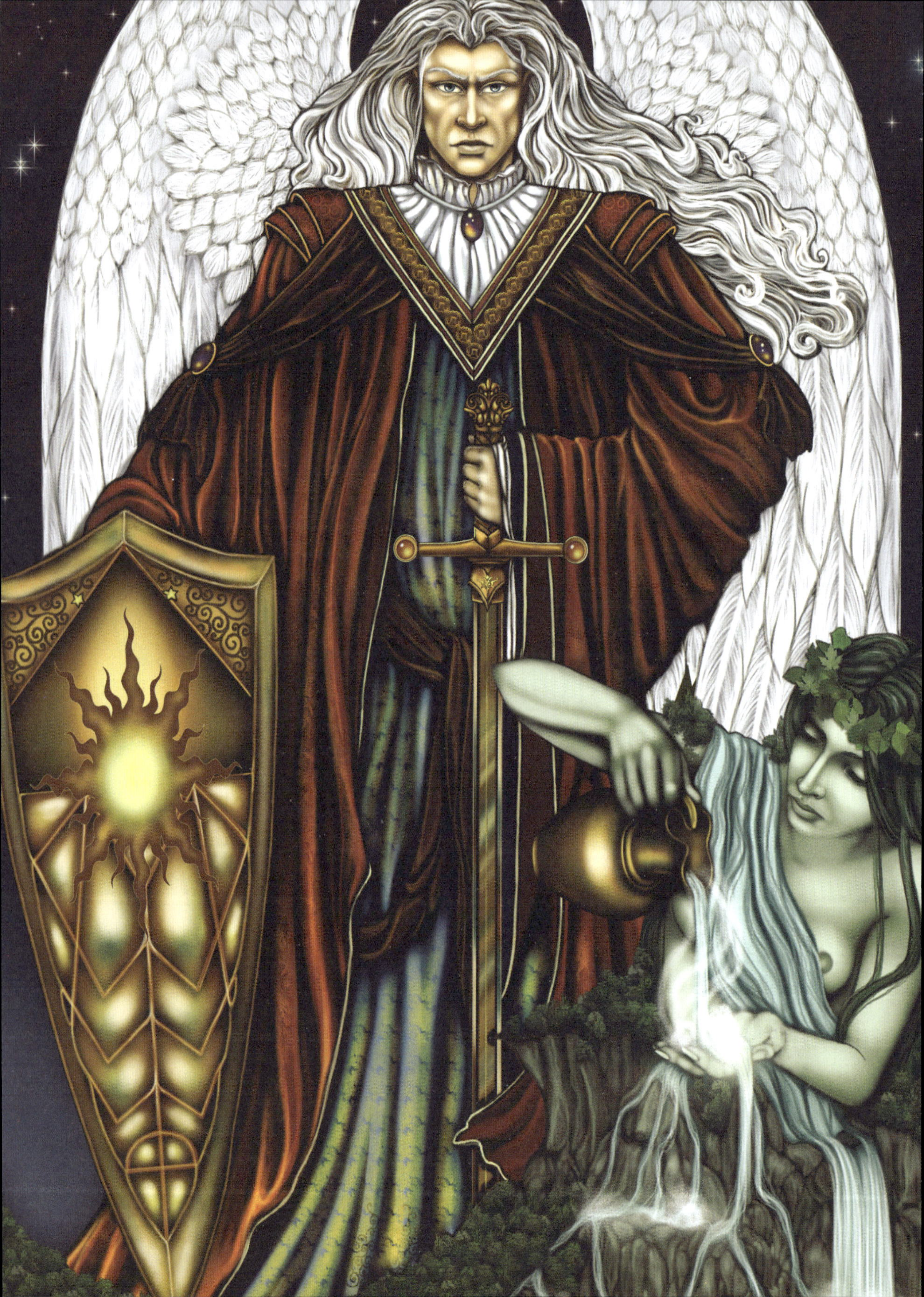

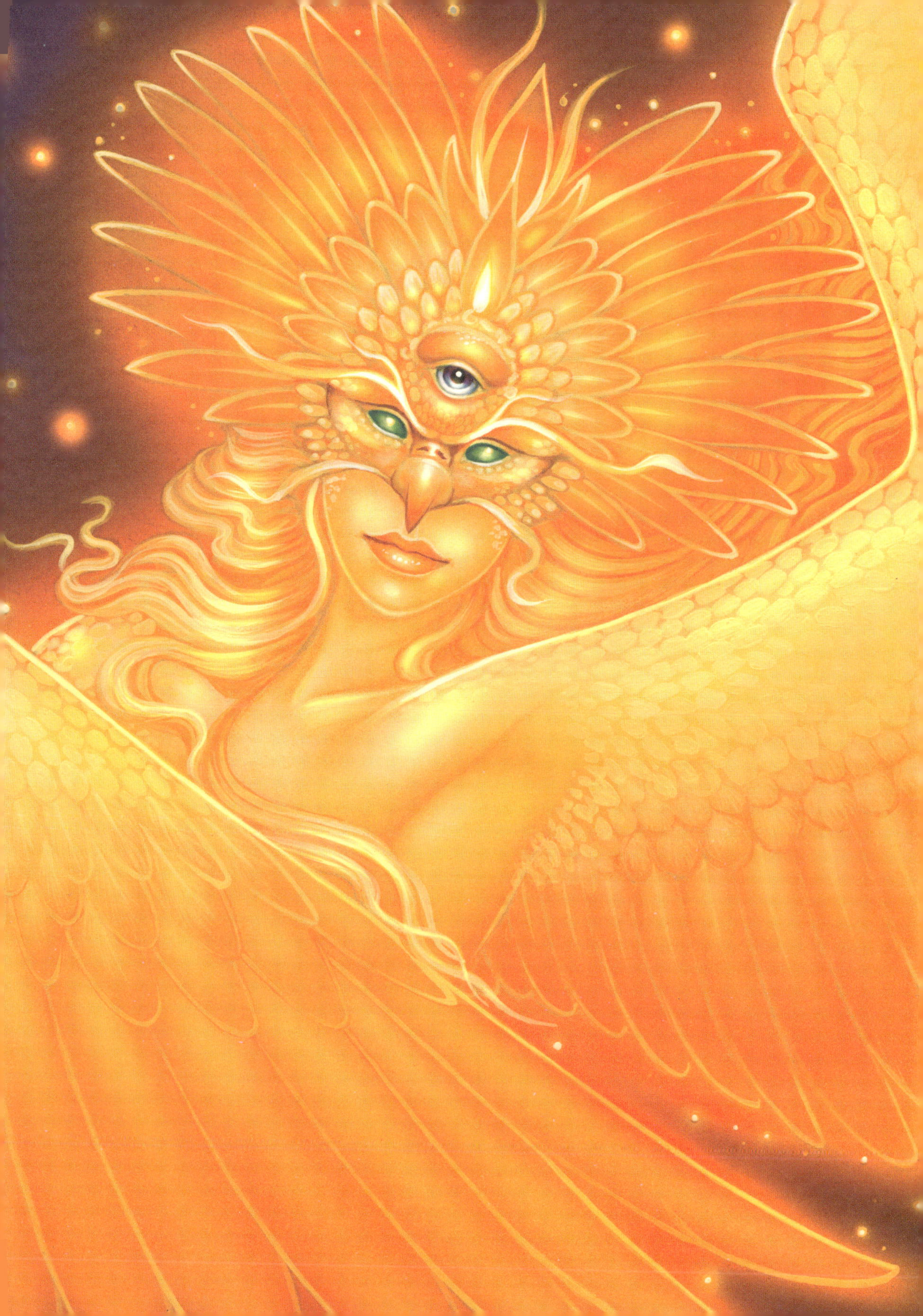

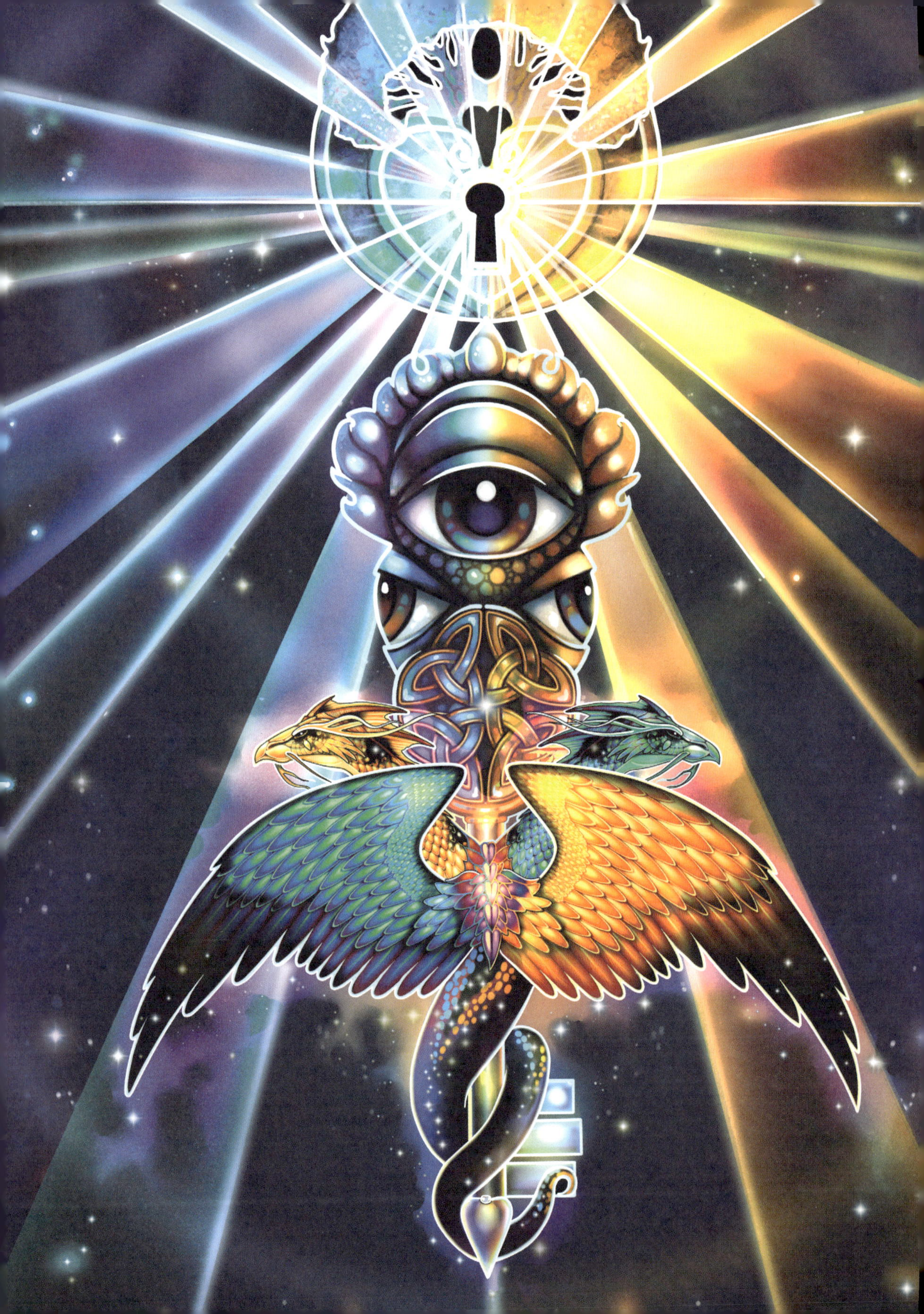